From our Kitchen to Yours

ALL-TIME-FAVORITE RECIPES From
ALABAMA
COOKS

Dedication

For every cook who wants to create amazing
recipes from the great state of Alabama.

Appreciation

Thanks to all our Alabama cooks who shared their
delightful and delicious recipes with us!

Gooseberry Patch
An imprint of Globe Pequot
64 South Main Street
Essex, CT 06426
www.gooseberrypatch.com
1 800 854 6673

Copyright 2024, Gooseberry Patch
978-162093-555-2

Do you have a tried & true recipe...tip, craft or
memory that you'd like to see featured in a
Gooseberry Patch cookbook? Visit our website at
www.gooseberrypatch.com and follow the easy steps
to submit your favorite family recipe.

Or send them to us at:

Gooseberry Patch
PO Box 812
Columbus, OH 43216-0812

Don't forget to include the number of servings your
recipe makes, plus your name, address, phone
number and email address. If we select your recipe,
your name will appear right along with it...and you'll
receive a FREE copy of the book!

ALABAMA COOKS

ICONIC ALABAMA

Alabama...the Heart of Dixie, and heart it has! Known for its southern hospitality, Mardi Gras, civil rights movement, NASA, heartland cuisine and acclaimed music, Alabama is rich in its culture, history and beautiful landscapes.

From its white beaches to its forests, mountains, and foothills of the Appalachians, Alabama is America's 28th largest exporter of agricultural products like cotton, peanuts and pecans!

Known for its delicious cuisines which are deep–rooted in Alabama's culture and history, local southerners and visitors alike, look forward to white BBQ sauce, tomato pie, fried green tomatoes, boiled peanuts, pecan pie, sweet tea, shrimp and grits, and smothered southern pork chops.

Like the state bird, the Yellowhammer, the official state dessert, the "Lane Cake" also appeared to be fowl-friendly when the cake debuted in the classic novel "To Kill a Mockingbird." This yummy layered sponge cake is topped with a delicious combination of coconut, raisins, pecans, and bourbon for its frosting.

Inside this cookbook you will find mouthwatering, tried & true recipes from cooks all around the great state of Alabama, including Grilled Chicken & White BBQ Sauce, Italian Fried Green Tomatoes, Southern Pork Chalupas, Granny's Jalapeño Cornbread, Raisin Rocks and Dixie-Lane Cake!

From our Kitchen to Yours

OUR STORY

Back in 1984, our families were neighbors in little Delaware, Ohio. With small children, we wanted to do what we loved and stay home with the kids too. We had always shared a love of home cooking and so, **Gooseberry Patch** was born.

Almost immediately, we found a connection with our customers and it wasn't long before these friends started sharing recipes. Since then we've enjoyed publishing hundreds of cookbooks with your tried & true recipes.

We know we couldn't have done it without our friends all across the country and we look forward to continuing to build a community with you. Welcome to the **Gooseberry Patch** family!

JoAnn & Vickie

TABLE OF CONTENTS

CHAPTER ONE

COVERED BRIDGE
Breakfasts

ENJOY THESE TASTY BREAKFAST RECIPES THAT BRING YOU TO THE TABLE WITH A HEARTY "GOOD MORNING!" AND CARRY YOU THROUGH THE DAY TO TACKLE WHATEVER COMES YOUR WAY.

SAUSAGE MUFFINS

CAROLYN BRITTON
MILLRY, AL

These are great to make ahead and freeze individually. Just heat and serve for a quick breakfast or snack.

1 lb. ground turkey
  sausage
1/4 c. butter
5-oz. jar sharp
  pasteurized process
  cheese spread
1/4 t. garlic powder
6 English muffins, split

In a skillet over medium heat, brown sausage; drain. Add butter, cheese and garlic powder; mix and cook until cheese melts. Spread sausage mixture on 6 English muffin halves. Place on an ungreased baking sheet and bake at 350 degrees for 15 minutes, or until heated through. Top with remaining halves of English muffins.

Makes 6.

CRUSTLESS MINI QUICHES

PHYLLIS FOLKES
ASHFORD, AL

These little quiches are great for a light breakfast, lunch or supper.

2 eggs, beaten
1/2 c. half-and-half
1/2 c. mayonnaise
2 T. all-purpose flour
1-1/2 t. seasoned salt
1/8 t. pepper
8-oz. pkg. shredded
  Swiss cheese
1 c. bacon, crisply cooked
  and crumbled
1/4 c. onion, finely
  chopped

Combine all ingredients in a large bowl; mix well. Divide mixture among 12 greased muffin cups, filling cups 1/2 full. Bake at 350 degrees for 20 to 22 minutes, until lightly golden and a knife tip inserted in the center comes out clean.

Makes one dozen.

JOHNNY APPLESEED TOAST

REBEKAH SPOONER
HUNTSVILLE, AL

I'm a teacher, and we make this every fall to celebrate Johnny Appleseed with our little ones in September.

Spread each slice of bread with one teaspoon of butter. Cover each bread slice with an apple slice; drizzle with one teaspoon honey and sprinkle with cinnamon. Place topped bread slices on an ungreased baking sheet. Broil on high for one to 2 minutes, or until toasted and golden.

Makes 4 servings.

4 slices cinnamon-raisin bread
1-1/2 T. butter, divided
1 Gala apple, cored and sliced
4 t. honey
1 t. cinnamon

KITCHEN TIP

Save your hard cheese rinds to add to broths, soups, and stews. Allowing rinds to simmer in the liquid for 20 to 30 minutes really takes the flavor up a notch!

CHICKEN & ASPARAGUS QUICHE

MELISSA KNIGHT
ATHENS, AL

My mother's wonderful quiche recipe is perfect for Christmas brunch!

2 9-inch pie crusts
2 T. butter
2 T. olive oil
1 T. garlic, minced
1 onion, chopped
1 bunch asparagus,
  trimmed and cut into
  1-inch pieces
2 boneless, skinless
  chicken breasts, diced
3 eggs, beaten
1 c. half-and-half
1 t. dry mustard
salt and pepper to taste
2 c. shredded Monterey
  Jack cheese, divided

Place pie crusts in two 9" pie plates; bake at 450 degrees for 10 to 12 minutes, until lightly golden. Meanwhile, in a large skillet, melt butter and olive oil over medium heat. Sauté garlic, onion and asparagus for 5 to 7 minutes, until asparagus is crisp-tender. With a slotted spoon, remove vegetables from skillet, leaving as much of the butter mixture as possible. Add chicken to skillet; sauté for 7 to 8 minutes, until fully cooked. Remove skillet from heat. In a bowl, whisk together remaining ingredients except cheeses. Sprinkle 1/2 cup cheese in each pie crust. Layer half the chicken in each crust, followed by half the veggies and half the egg mixture. Top with remaining cheese. Bake, uncovered, at 375 degrees for 30 to 35 minutes.

Makes 2 quiches; each serves 4 to 6.

SAUSAGE-CHEESE BALLS

**BELINDA BURGESS
ASHVILLE, AL**

*Both my grandmother and my mother made these yummy tidbits. I
can remember having them for breakfast any day of the week as well
as holidays. I have often gone back to this recipe when needing an
addition to breakfast or brunch or an appetizer.*

In a large bowl, combine uncooked sausage and
remaining ingredients. With your hands, mix well and
form into one-inch balls. Place on a greased baking
sheet. Bake at 350 degrees for 25 minutes, or until
golden and sausage is no longer pink.

Makes about 3 dozen.

1 lb. ground pork
  sausage
1/4 c. water
2 c. biscuit baking mix
2 c. shredded Cheddar
  cheese

JUST FOR FUN

French settlers arrived in Mobile,
Alabama in 1699 where it became the
home of Mardi Gras in 1703.

SAUSAGE & GRITS CASSEROLE

ARLENE GRIMM
DECATUR, AL

I got this recipe from a dear friend, and it's so versatile. Add some of your favorite vegetables, use a different type of cheese, or add ham or bacon instead of sausage...it's delicious no matter what!

1 lb. spicy ground pork breakfast sausage

1/2 c. onion, finely chopped

1 c. quick-cooking grits, uncooked

2-1/4 c. shredded sharp Cheddar cheese, divided

3 eggs, beaten

2 T. butter

1-1/2 T. milk

1/2 t. salt

1/4 t. pepper

Brown sausage and onion in a large skillet over medium heat; drain and set aside. Cook grits according to package directions. In a bowl, combine sausage mixture, grits, 2 cups cheese and remaining ingredients; mix well. Pour into a greased 13"x9" baking pan; cover loosely with aluminum foil. Bake at 350 degrees for 50 to 55 minutes. Remove foil and sprinkle with remaining cheese. Let stand until cheese melts, about 2 to 3 minutes.

Serves 8 to 10.

CHRISTMAS EVE BRUNCH

JANICE FRY
HOOVER, AL

This recipe was given to me many years ago by a dear older lady from our church. At the time, I was a young bride and was nervous about cooking anything, much less making a holiday brunch dish. However, I tried it and, surprise! I made it for our first Christmas together. It's easy and good! Now, 45 years later, I'm still making it every Christmas, to serve our five children & their spouses and nine hungry grandchildren.

Arrange Canadian bacon slices in a lightly greased 13"x9" baking pan; top with Swiss cheese slices. Break eggs into pan, spacing evenly. Carefully pour cream over eggs. Bake, uncovered, at 450 degrees for 10 minutes. Sprinkle with Parmesan cheese, pepper and paprika. Bake an additional 8 to 10 minutes, until set. Sprinkle with parsley; let stand 10 minutes before serving.

Makes 6 to 8 servings.

- 12 slices Canadian bacon
- 12 slices Swiss cheese
- 1 doz. eggs
- 1 c. whipping cream
- 1/3 c. grated Parmesan cheese pepper and paprika to taste
- Garnish: chopped fresh parsley

JUST FOR FUN

Saturn V, a rocket which sent nine crewed flights to the moon and launched the first American space station, was built in Huntsville, Alabama. It was first launched in 1967 and was about the height of a 36-story building and weighed about the same as 400 elephants!

SAUSAGE & EGG BRUNCH CASEROLE

ANNETTE CERAVOLO
BIRMINGHAM, AL

My mother-in-law made this overnight dish for her family and I now make it for my family. She loved to cook, and I always think of her when I make it.

6 eggs, beaten

2 c. milk

1 t. dry mustard

1 lb. ground pork breakfast sausage, browned and drained

6 slices bread, crusts removed and cubed

1 c. shredded medium or sharp Cheddar cheese

Optional: salt and pepper to taste

In a large bowl, whisk together eggs, milk and mustard. Add remaining ingredients; stir well. Transfer to a greased 9"x9" baking pan; cover and refrigerate for 8 to 12 hours. Uncover; bake at 350 degrees for 45 minutes to one hour, until heated through.

Serves 4 to 6.

FRIENDSHIP APPLE CRUMPETS

CHERRY LAIRD
MAXWELL AFB, AL

This is a recipe shared with me by a friend... it's so good, I make it as often as I can!

Combine all ingredients except biscuits in a large bowl. Toss until apples are well coated; set aside. Reserve 4 biscuits for another recipe. Flatten remaining biscuits to 1/4-inch thick. Spray a muffin tin with non-stick vegetable spray or line with paper liners. Lay biscuits at over muffin opening; spoon apple mixture onto each biscuit. Use a spoon to gently push biscuit and mixture into muffin cup. Gather dough and pinch to seal, covering apples as much as possible. Sprinkle with additional brown sugar blend and cinnamon, if desired. Bake at 375 degrees for 10 to 15 minutes. Cool slightly before serving.

Makes one dozen.

3 Gala apples, cored and chopped

2 T. vanilla extract

2 T. powdered low-calorie brown sugar blend for baking

2 t. cinnamon

1/2 t. allspice

2 16.3-oz. tubes refrigerated jumbo whole-wheat low-fat biscuits, divided

APPLE CIDER SYRUP

BEN GOTHARD
JEMISON, AL

Treat yourself...this warm syrup is yummy drizzled over pancakes, waffers and homemade biscuits!

1/2 c. sugar
1/2 c. light brown sugar, packed
2 T. cornstarch
1/4 t. cinnamon
1/4 t. nutmeg
2 c. apple cider
1 T. lemon juice
1/4 c. butter, softened

In a saucepan, mix together sugars, cornstarch and spices. Pour in apple cider and lemon juice, mixing well. Cook over medium heat until thickened and boiling, stirring constantly. Boil and stir for one minute; remove from heat. Stir in butter before serving.

Makes 14 servings.

CREAMY EGG BAKE

JO ANN
GOOSEBERRY PATCH

Everyone gets their own little breakfast portion...just add some hot buttered toast!

2 t. butter, softened
3 T. whipping cream
8 eggs
salt and pepper to taste
4 t. fresh chives, minced
4 t. grated Parmesan cheese

Spread butter inside 4 ramekins or custard cups. Divide cream evenly among ramekins. Crack 2 eggs into each ramekin, keeping yolks unbroken. Season with salt and pepper; sprinkle with chives and cheese. Set ramekins on a baking sheet. Bake at 325 degrees for 12 to 15 minutes, until egg whites have set and yolks are still soft. Remove from oven. Let stand for a few minutes before serving.

Makes 4 servings.

MOLLY'S MUFFINS

MARY HUGHES
TALLADEGA, AL

My sister Molly and I came up with this recipe years ago and it's always been a family favorite!

In a bowl, blend egg, butter or oil and milk; set aside. In another bowl, blend flour, baking powder, 1/2 cup sugar, salt strawberries and chcolate chips. Add egg mixture to flour mixture; blend with a spatula but do not overmix. Spoon batter into 8 greased muffin cups, filling 2/3 full. In a small cup, sprinkle remaining sugar over batter. Bake at 375 degrees for 20 to 25 minutes.

Makes 8 muffins.

1 egg, lightly beaten

2 T. butter, softened, or oil

3/4 c. milk

1 c. all-purpose flour

1 t. baking powder

1/2 c. plus 2 tablespoons sugar, divided

1/2 t. salt

1-1/2 c. strawberries, diced

1/3 c. mini chocolate chips

DINNERTIME CONVERSATION

In 1836 Alabama was the first state to declare Christmas a legal holiday. In 1870, The United States federal government eventually declared December 25, a public holiday.

MEXICALI BREAKFAST POTATOES

VICKIE
GOOSEBERRY PATCH

This hearty potato dish is a wonderful change from ordinary hashbrowns! It's become a tailgating brunch favorite for our family & friends. Garnish with sour cream and a sprinkle of cheese.

32-oz. pkg. frozen diced potatoes
1/4 c. onion, diced
1/4 c. red pepper, diced
1/4 c. canned diced green chiles
1 T. Dijon mustard
1-1/4 t. ground cumin
1-1/4 t. salt
1 t. pepper
1/2 t. cayenne pepper
1 T. canola oil

In a large bowl, combine all ingredients except oil; mix well and set aside. Add oil to a large skillet; heat over medium heat. Add potato mixture to skillet. Cook, stirring often, for 12 to 15 minutes, until potatoes are golden.

Makes 8 servings.

JUST FOR FUN

There are 11 historic covered bridges that still reamin in Alabama. The longest covered bridge is the Swann Covered Bridge at 324 feet long!

ANNETTE'S BREAKFAST PIE

ANNETTE CERAVOLO
HOOVER, AL

A great make-ahead dish for overnight guests, or just anytime you want to treat your family to a wonderful breakfast! Don't be tempted to use precooked bacon...the crispy bacon makes all the difference in this scrumptious dish.

Cook bacon in a large skillet over medium heat until crisp; drain on paper towels. Meanwhile, beat eggs in a large bowl. Add remaining ingredients except paprika; mix well. Spoon into a greased 10" glass pie plate; sprinkle with crumbled bacon and paprika. Cover and refrigerate for at least 8 hours. Place the cold dish, uncovered, in a cold oven. Bake, uncovered, at 350 degrees for 35 minutes, or until hashbrowns are tender and eggs are set. Cut into wedges.

Serves 6 to 8.

12 slices bacon

5 eggs, beaten

10-oz. pkg. refrigerated shredded hashbrowns

1/2 c. shredded Swiss cheese

1/4 c. green onion, chopped

4 drops hot pepper sauce

1/2 t. salt

1/8 t. pepper

paprika to taste

PEAR PANCAKE

MARY HUGHES
TALLADEGA, AL

Top each slice with a sprinkling of powdered sugar...yum!

**4 pears, cored, peeled
and sliced**
**1/4 c. brown sugar,
packed**
1/4 c. lemon juice
1 c. all-purpose flour
1 c. milk
3 T. sugar
1 t. vanilla extract
1/4 t. salt
3 eggs, beaten

Combine pears, brown sugar and lemon juice; stir well. Pour into a 12" skillet; sauté until pears are golden, about 5 minutes. Remove from heat; set aside. Place flour in a large mixing bowl; set aside. Whisk remaining ingredients together; pour into flour, mix well. Pour batter into an ungreased 12" oven-proof skillet; bake at 425 degrees until golden and puffy, about 25 minutes. Spoon warm pear mixture into the center before serving.

Serves 4.

CHILI RELLENO CASSEROLE

MICHELLE POWELL
VALLEY, AL

*A slow-cooker casserole that's ideal for a breakfast with family
& friends. For a real kick, add some chopped jalapenõs to taste!*

**1-lb. pkg. ground
breakfast sausage,
browned and drained**
**4-oz. can diced green
chiles**
1 onion, diced
1 green pepper, diced
**2-1/2 c. shredded
Monterey Jack or
Pepper Jack cheese**
18 eggs, beaten
**Garnish: sour cream,
salsa**

In a greased slow cooker, layer half each sausage, chiles, onion, pepper and cheese. Repeat layering with remaining ingredients except eggs and garnish, ending with cheese. Pour beaten eggs over top. Cover and cook on low setting for 7 to 8 hours. Serve with sour cream and salsa.

Serves 12.

PEANUT BUTTER & CHOCOLATE HAZELNUT FRENCH TOAST

CONSTANCE LEWIS
FLORENCE, AL

My most requested dish...who can resist the taste of peanut butter & chocolate?

Use bread, peanut butter and chocolate hazelnut spread to make 2 sandwiches; set aside. In a bowl, whisk together eggs and milk. Dip each sandwich into egg mixture. Melt butter in a non-stick skillet over medium heat. Add sandwiches to skillet and cook until golden, about 2 to 3 minutes on each side. Top with sliced banana.

Serves 2.

4 slices white bread
1/2 c. creamy peanut butter
2 T. chocolate hazelnut spread
3 eggs, beaten
1/4 c. milk
2 T. butter
Garnish: banana

JUST FOR FUN

According to a recent study, Alabama has the highest percentage of followers for college football.

MONKEY COFFEE CAKE

MARY HUGHES
TALLADEGA, AL

Banana bread and coffee cake...the best of both worlds!

2 c. all-purpose flour

3 t. baking powder

1 teaspoon ground cinnamon

1 t. salt

3 ripe bananas, peeled and mashed

1/2 c. unsalted butter, softened to room temperature

1 c. granulated sugar

2 large eggs

1 t. vanilla

1 c. almond milk

CRUMB MIX:

1/2 c. cold unsalted butter, cut into small cubes

1 c. all purpose flour

1 c. packed light brown sugar

1/2 c. granulated sugar

1 t. ground cinnamon

Prepare a 9" x 13" baking dish with butter. Prepare crumb mixture and set aside. In a large bowl, whisk together flour, baking powder, cinnamon, and salt. In a separate bowl, mix softened butter on medium speed until creamy, add sugar and mix for another minute. Then without overmixing, fold in eggs, vanilla and mashed bananas. Turn the mixer down to low, and alternate mixing in milk and flour until all ingredients are combined. Pour half of the cake mixture into the prepared baking dish. Top with ¼ of the crumb mixture. Pour the remaining cake mixture on top of that layer and top evenly with the remaining crumb topping. Bake at 350-degrees for 50 to 55 minutes, until a toothpick comes out clean.

Makes 6 to 8 servings.

Crumb Mixture:
In a large bowl, use your hands or two forks to crumble together cold butter, flour, sugars, and cinnamon until the mixture resembles a crumbly topping.

BAKED BLUEBERRY PANCAKE

BETHANY SCOTT
HUNTSVILLE, AL

A breakfast dish that is easy to make and is requested often. Kids both young and old love this!

In a 425-degree oven, melt butter in a 9" pie plate; remove from oven and set aside. Mix flour, eggs, milk and blueberries together, leaving batter a bit lumpy. Pour batter into pie plate. Bake for 20 minutes, or until puffy and golden. Cut into wedges. Serve immediately with maple syrup.

Makes 2 servings.

4 T. butter
1/2 c. all-purpose flour
1/2 c. milk
2 eggs
1/4 c. bluberries
Garnish: maple syrup

CINNAMON-GINGER TOASTED PECAN WAFFLES

CONSTANCE LEWIS
FLORENCE, AL

These are delicious topped with maple syrup, chopped pecans or fruit!

Combine flour, cinnamon, ginger, pecans and salt. Heat molasses and butter until butter melts. Remove from heat and stir in baking soda. Add buttermilk and egg, and then add flour mixture. Cook in a preheated, oiled waffle iron until golden.

Makes 9 waffles.

2 c. all-purpose flour
1 t. cinnamon
1/2 t. ground ginger
1/2 c. pecans, finely
    chopped and toasted
1/2 t. salt
1 c. molasses
1/2 c. butter
1-1/2 t. baking soda
1 c. buttermilk
1 egg

IT'S GOUDA QUICHE

**CONSTANCE LEWIS
FLORENCE, AL**

Made with shredded gouda cheese this quiche is my most requested recipe!

- 1/2 lb. bacon
- 3/4 c. white onion, chopped
- 8 eggs
- 2-1/4 c. milk
- 1-1/2 c. biscuit baking mix
- 1/2 c. shredded Gouda cheese
- 1/4 c. fresh spinach, chopped
- 1/2 t. salt
- 1/2 t. pepper

In a skillet over medium heat, cook bacon until crisp. Set aside bacon on paper towels to drain, reserving drippings. Sauté onion in drippings. Grease a 13"x9" baking pan with remaining drippings. Layer crumbled bacon and onion in pan; set aside. Beat eggs in a large bowl; whisk in milk. Add biscuit mix, cheese and spinach, salt and pepper; stir well. Pour mixture into pan. Bake at400 degrees for 15 minutes. Reduce oven to 350 degrees and continue baking another 30 minutes, or until a knife tip inserted in center come out clean. Let stand for 10 minutes; cut into wedges. Serve warm.

Makes 6 servings.

GOOD-TIME SAUSAGE GRAVY

MARY HUGHES
TALLADEGA, AL

My family has been gathering for years on Saturday mornings (or afternoons) for this yummy sausage gravy breakfast.

Brown sausage in a large skillet over medium heat. Using a slotted spoon, remove sausage to a papertowel-lined plate. Add water and milk to drippings in skillet; bring to a simmer. Gradually add flour and seasonings; cook and stir until blended. For a thicker consistency, add more flour. Return sausage to skillet; stir until thickened. Serve hot over warm biscuits.

Serves 8 to 12.

1 lb. ground pork
  breakfast sausage
5 c. water
7 c. milk
1-1/2 c. all-purpose flour
2 T. salt
1 T. pepper
country biscuits

CAN'T-FAIL BISCUITS

ARLENE GRIMM
DECATUR, AL

A really easy biscuit recipe. Tasty when spread with jams or honey.

Mix together flour and whipping cream; roll out on a floured board and cut out biscuits with a round cutter. Place on a greased baking sheet and bake 10 to 12 minutes at 375 degrees.

Makes about one dozen.

2 c. self-rising flour
1 c. whipping cream

CHRISTMAS CASSEROLE

**BETHANY SCOTT
HUNTSVILLE, AL**

Quick & easy to prepare the evening before, then just pop it in the oven in the morning!

1/3 c. green pepper, diced
1/3 c. red pepper, diced
1/3 c. onion, diced
1-1/2 lb. ground sausage, browned
2-1/2 c. plain croutons
2 c. shredded Cheddar cheese, divided
6 to 8 eggs
2-3/4 c. milk, divided
1/2 t. salt
1/8 t. pepper
10-3/4 oz. can cream of mushroom soup

Brown sausage with peppers and onions. Arrange croutons in a greased 13"x9" baking pan. Top with 1-1/2 cups shredded cheese, then with sausage mixture. Blend together eggs and 2-1/4 cups milk in a large bowl; add salt and pepper and mix well. Pour egg mixture over sausage; cover with aluminum foil and refrigerate overnight. Just before baking, blend together remaining milk and soup and pour over egg mixture; sprinkle with remaining cheese. Bake at 350 degrees for one to 1-1/2 hours.

Serves 8.

KITCHEN TIP

Extend the lifespan of washed herbs and greens by placing them in zipper-locked bags with damp paper towels in-between layers and the seals left slightly open.

CINNAMON BREAKFAST BIRTHDAY CAKE

MARY HUGHES
TALLADEGA, AL

Our family loves cinnamon rolls, but I don't always have time to make them. This cake is quick to make and I always have the ingredients on hand. Perfect for breakfast or brunch...delicious at lunch with a hearty soup too.

In a large bowl, combine 3 cups flour, sugar, baking powder, salt, milk, eggs and vanilla; mix well. Slowly pour in melted butter; stir. Pour batter into a greased bundt pan. In a separate bowl, mix together softened butter, remaining flour, brown sugar and cinnamon. Drop mixture over batter and swirl into batter with a knife. Bake at 350 degrees for 30 to 40 minutes, or until a toothpick inserted in the center comes out clean. Cool; spread with Cream Cheese Frosting.

Serves 10 to 12.

Cream Cheese Frosting:
Stir together cream cheese and butter until smooth. Add extract, salt and powdered sugar. Thin to desired consistency by adding milk 1 tablesppon at a time.

- 3 c. plus 2 T. all-purpose flour, divided
- 1 c. sugar
- 4 t. baking powder
- 1/4 t. salt
- 1-1/2 c. milk
- 2 eggs, beaten
- 2 t. vanilla extract
- 1/2 c. butter, melted
- 1/2 c. butter, softened
- 1 c. brown sugar, packed
- 1 T. cinnamon

CREAM CHEESE FROSTING

- 4-oz. pkg. cream cheese, room temperature
- 4 T. unsalted butter, softened
- 1 c. powdered sugar
- 1 t. vanilla extract
- pinch of salt
- 1/4 c milk (more if necessary)

CHAPTER TWO

SUPERSPEEDWAY

Salads & Sides

TOSS TOGETHER GREAT TASTE AND
HEALTHY GOODNESS TO MAKE
FRESH, SATISFYING AND TASTY
SALADS AND SIDES THAT ARE
PACKED WITH FULL-ON FLAVOR.

CRUNCHY BACON COLESLAW

CONSTANCE LEWIS
FLORENCE, AL

This delicious coleslaw is sure to be invited whenever burgers or barbecue are on the menu.

3/4 c. mayonnaise
1 T. sugar
1-1/2 t. cider vinegar
4 c. green cabbage, shredded
1 c. red cabbage, shredded
4 slices bacon, crisply cooked and crumbled, or 1/2 c. real bacon bits
1/2 c. chopped peanuts

Mix mayonnaise, sugar and vinegar in a large bowl. Add remaining ingredients; mix lightly. Cover and chill until serving time.

Makes 8 to 10 servings.

SPICY BROCCOLI PASTA

MARY BETH SCHANCK
DOTHAN, AL

I came up with this recipe to get my son to eat vegetables with his much-loved pasta. It makes a really tasty dish!

16-oz. pkg. bowtie pasta, uncooked
1 bunch broccoli, cut into bite-size flowerets
1/4 c. olive oil
1/4 c. lemon juice
1 to 2 T. butter, melted
red pepper flakes
salt and pepper to taste
Garnish: shredded Parmesan cheese

Cook pasta according to package instructions, adding broccoli during the last 3 minutes of cooking time. Drain, reserving 1/2 cup cooking liquid. In a large bowl, combine olive oil, lemon juice, butter and seasonings. Add reserved liquid to oil mixture. Add broccoli and cooked pasta; toss to coat well. Serve with Parmesan cheese.

Makes 4 servings.

MEXICAN ROASTED CAULIFLOWER

MICHELLE POWELL
VALLEY, AL

A tasty veggie side to serve with tacos or enchiladas. It's a tasty alternative to refried beans & rice that even my cauliflower-haters love. So quick and tasty...you'll make it often!

Mix oil, garlic and spices in a large bowl. Add the cauliflower; toss to coat. Spread in an ungreased shallow roasting pan. Bake, uncovered, at 325 degrees for one hour and 15 minutes, stirring occasionally. Remove from oven. Drizzle with lime juice; sprinkle with cilantro and toss well. Serve warm.

Makes 6 servings.

3 T. olive oil
3 cloves garlic, minced
1 T. chili powder, or to taste
1/2 t. ground cumin
1 lb. cauliflower, cut into bite-size flowerets
juice of 1 lime
1/4 c. fresh cilantro, chopped

FIESTA CORN CASSEROLE

MARY JEFFERSON RABON
MOBILE, AL

I was given this recipe 20 years ago. It is a favorite side dish for Thanksgiving and Christmas for my family!

Cook rice according to package directions; stir in butter, corn and soup. Stir in one cup of cheese, or more as desired. Transfer to a lightly greased 13"x9" baking pan. Bake, uncovered, at 325 degrees for 25 minutes, or until bubbly and cheese is melted. Top with remaining cheese and bake for 5 more minutes.

Serves 8 to 10.

5-oz. pkg. long-cooking yellow rice, uncooked
1/4 c. butter, melted
2 11-oz. cans sweet corn and diced peppers
10-3/4 oz. can cream of celery soup
8-oz. pkg. shredded sharp Cheddar cheese, divided

CHEESY CAULIFLOWER CASSEROLE

MICHELLE POWELL
VALLEY, AL

This easy side tastes like a loaded baked potato!

2 lbs. fresh or frozen cauliflower flowerets

16-oz. pkg. shredded Colby Jack cheese, divided

8-oz. container plain Greek yogurt

1/4 c. milk

1 bunch green onions, thinly sliced

6 slices bacon, crisply cooked and crumbled

1 clove garlic, pressed

salt and pepper to taste

Add cauliflower to a saucepan of boiling water. Cook for 8 to 14 minutes, just until tender. Drain well; mash slightly with a potato masher. Meanwhile, in a bowl, blend 3 cups cheese, yogurt and milk. Stir in onions, bacon and garlic. Add cheese mixture to cauliflower; stir well. Season with salt and pepper. Spoon into a greased 2-quart casserole dish; top with remaining cheese. Cover with aluminum foil. Bake at 350 degrees for 25 minutes. Uncover; bake until cheese is bubbly, about 5 minutes.

Makes 6 to 8 servings.

SCALLOPED SWEET POTATOES & APPLES

MICHELLE POWELL
VALLEY, AL

Great with ham!

2 sweet potatoes, boiled, peeled and sliced

2 tart apples, peeled, cored and sliced

1/2 c. brown sugar, packed

1/4 c. butter, sliced

1 t. salt

Layer half the potatoes in a buttered 13"x9" baking pan. Layer half the apple slices. Sprinkle with half the sugar; dot with half the butter. Repeat with remaining ingredients. Bake, uncovered, at 350 degrees for one hour.

Makes 6 servings.

BLUE CHEESE SLAW

MELISSA KNIGHT
ATHENS, AL

What's a cookout without the perfect coleslaw? Here is a scrumptious and easy twist on typical slaw recipes.

In a large bowl, combine cabbage and carrots. In a smaller bowl, combine remaining ingredients except cheese and parsley. Pour mixture over cabbage; toss well to coat. Stir in cheese and parsley. Cover and refrigerate for at least 2 hours before serving.

Makes 10 to 12 servings.

2 c. green cabbage, shredded

2 c. red cabbage, shredded

2 c. carrots, peeled and shredded

3/4 c. mayonnaise

1 T. Dijon mustard

1-1/2 t. dry mustard

1-1/2 t. seasoning salt

1-1/2 t. cider vinegar

salt and pepper to taste

3/4 c. crumbled blue cheese

2 T. fresh parsley, minced

PRESENTATION

Prepare any triffle or layered recipe into clear plastic drinking cups. Serving individualized snacks, dips and desserts this way is fun and easy for your guests!

BROCCOLI & RICOTTA-STUFFED SHELLS

CRYSTAL INESTROZA
ATHENS, AL

Any leftover Alfredo sauce may be spooned over grilled chicken breasts, which go well with this dish.

- 12-oz. pkg. jumbo pasta shells, uncooked
- 16-oz. container ricotta cheese
- 1/4 c. shredded Parmesan cheese
- 1 egg, beaten
- 1 T. garlic, minced
- 1 t. Italian seasoning
- 1/4 t. pepper
- 10-oz. pkg. frozen chopped broccoli, thawed and well drained
- 2 15-oz. jars Alfredo sauce
- 1 c. water

Cook pasta according to package directions. Drain and rinse with cold water. Meanwhile, in a bowl, mix remaining ingredients except sauce and water. Stuff each shell with one tablespoon of ricotta mixture. Arrange shells in a lightly greased 13"x9" baking pan; set aside. Combine sauce and water in a saucepan; heat over medium-low heat until warmed through. Ladle sauce over shells, covering all shells with sauce. Reserve any remaining sauce for another use. Cover pan with aluminum foil. Bake at 350 degrees for 40 to 45 minutes, until hot and bubbly.

Serves 6.

DINNERTIME CONVERSATION

Alabama is the only place in the world where all three resources needed to make steel can be found close to each other. In Birmingham, AL all the ingredients for steel are found in the same place.

LINDSEY'S SPICY RICE

LINDSEY WISE HOWARD
HOLLY POND, AL

I'm a college student on a budget, so I try to use up everything in my pantry before I go grocery shopping again. One night, I was left with rice, a can of spicy tomatoes and a little cheese, so I mixed them together. It was delicious! The cheese adds just the right amount of flavor and cools down the heat of the chiles.

In a saucepan over medium-high heat, bring water to a boil. Add rice and boil for 8 to 10 minutes; drain. Pour tomatoes into saucepan and mix together with rice; heat through. Cheese may be stirred into mixture or sprinkled over each serving.

Makes 2 to 4 servings.

1 c. water
1/2 to 3/4 c. shredded Cheddar cheese
1/2 c. quick-cooking rice, uncooked
10-oz. can diced tomatoes with green chiles

ROASTED SWEET ONIONS

MICHELLE POWELL
VALLEY, AL

These onions are excellent as a side, on a burger or in a salad. They're quick to fix and add so much flavor to any meal.

Place onion wedges in a slow cooker. Drizzle oil over onions; toss to coat well. Sprinkle with salt, pepper and thyme; stir and drizzle with vinegar. Cover and cook on high setting for 4 hours, or until onions are golden and very soft.

Serves 6.

4 sweet onions, cut into 8 wedges
1/4 c. olive oil
1-1/2 t. salt
1/2 t. pepper
2 t. dried thyme
2 T. balsamic vinegar

TOMATOES CREOLE

DONNA CLEMENT
DAPHNE, AL

*Living in New Orleans for years and then moving to southern
Alabama gave me a taste of some of the best dishes in America.
Southerners can really cook!*

1/2 c. fresh parsley,
  chopped

2 cloves garlic, chopped

6 tomatoes, sliced 1/4-
  inch thick

salt and pepper to taste

1/4 c. butter, sliced

1-1/4 c. seasoned dry
  bread crumbs

grated Parmesan
  cheese to taste

Mix together parsley and garlic in a small bowl; set aside. Arrange tomato slices in a buttered 13"x9" baking pan. Season tomatoes with salt and pepper; dot with butter. Sprinkle with parsley mixture, bread crumbs and Parmesan cheese. Bake, uncovered, at 350 degrees for 30 minutes, or until bubbly and golden.

Makes 4 to 6 servings.

COMFORTING CREAMED CORN

MICHELLE POWELL
VALLEY, AL

Greek yogurt adds creaminess and protein to this simple dish.

1 T. butter

4 c. corn, thawed if
  frozen

1/2 c. plain Greek
  yogurt

2 T. grated Parmesan
  cheese

1 t. dried basil

Melt butter in a non-stick skillet over medium heat; add corn. Cook for about 6 minutes, stirring occasionally, until tender. Reduce heat; stir in yogurt and cook for 4 minutes. Stir in cheese and basil just before serving.

Makes 8 servings.

HAWAIIAN BAKED BEANS

**DEBRA ELLIOTT
BIRMINGHAM, AL**

*My children love pineapple and baked beans, so I thought, "Why
not combine the two into a yummy side dish?" I created this recipe
25 years ago, and it's still a family favorite.*

In a bowl, whisk together pineapple juice, catsup
and mustard. Add brown sugar and mix well; stir in
pineapple chunks. Add beans; mix well. Spoon into a
greased 13"x9" baking pan. Bake, uncovered, at
350 degrees for 90 minutes, or until hot and bubbly.

Serves 8 to 12.

- 1-3/4 c. pineapple juice
- 1 c. catsup
- 1/2 c. mustard
- 1-1/2 c. dark brown sugar, packed
- 15-oz. can pineapple chunks, drained
- 4 15-1/2 oz. cans navy beans & bacon, drained and rinsed

BAKED BUTTERNUT SQUASH

**MARY KING
ASHVILLE, AL**

*I can still smell the cinnamon baking when my mother and grandmother
used to make this recipe. I have served this yummy squash to my husband,
and he loves it too. One medium butternut squash serves two, so it's simple
to double this recipe.*

Place squash halves cut-side down on an ungreased
baking sheet. Bake at 350 degrees for 15 to
20 minutes. Turn squash halves over; top each half
with one tablespoon butter, one to 2 tablespoons
brown sugar and one teaspoon cinnamon. Bake at
350 degrees for an additional 30 to 40 minutes, until
fork-tender.

Makes 2 servings.

- 1 butternut squash, halved and seeds removed
- 2 T. butter
- 2 to 4 T. brown sugar, packed
- 2 t. cinnamon

STEAKHOUSE BROCCOLI SPEARS

MICHELLE POWELL
VALLEY, AL

This savory sauce keeps for weeks in the fridge. Serve over steamed broccoli for a quick supper side.

1 bunch broccoli, cut
  into serving-size stalks
salt to taste
1/4 c. butter, melted
1/4 c. mayonnaise
1 T. prepared
  horseradish
1 T. onion, grated
1/4 t. salt
1/4 t. dry mustard
1/8 t. cayenne pepper

Peel broccoli stalks with a vegetable peeler, if desired. Add to a saucepan of boiling salted water over medium-high heat. Cook until crisp-tender, about 8 minutes. Meanwhile, combine remaining ingredients in a bowl; blend well. Drain broccoli; season lightly with salt. Serve topped with a spoonful of sauce.

Makes 6 servings.

DILLED PEAS & POTATOES

MICHELLE MARBERRY
VALLEY, AL

This dish tastes like summer to me. Love it with ham at Easter too!

1-1/2 lbs. new potatoes
2 c. green peas, shelled
2 T. butter, sliced
3/4 c. whipping cream
3 T. fresh dill, chopped
1 t. salt

Cover potatoes with water in a Dutch oven. Over medium-high heat, boil for 15 minutes, or until potatoes are nearly tender. Add peas. Cover and cook for 5 minutes, or until peas are tender. Drain. Stir in butter until melted; add remaining ingredients and mix gently. Serve immediately.

Makes 6 to 8 servings.

WALTER'S SMOKY POTATOES

LERRI BLOW
JEMISON, AL

I was given this recipe by a sweet man I used to work with. I made it just like he said, and it was amazing. The potatoes come out so tender, plus the green pepper and onion add a wonderful taste to the dish. You can also place everything in foil packets and cook them on the grill.

In a large bowl, combine potatoes, green pepper, onion and sausage. Sprinkle with garlic powder, salt and pepper. Add 5 tablespoons butter; mix well to coat. Fold in remaining butter. Transfer mixture to 2 lightly greased 8"x8" baking pans. Bake, covered, at 400 degrees for one hour, or until potatoes are tender.

Serves 8 to 10.

8 to 10 baking potatoes, cubed

1 green pepper, diced

1 onion, diced

14-oz. smoked pork sausage ring, sliced

2 t. garlic powder

1/2 t. salt

1 t. pepper

10 T. butter, melted and divided

KITCHEN TIP

Use the empty half of an egg shell to extract pieces of cracked shells that have ended up in the bowl. The cracked shell is almost magnetic and will pull small shell pieces into it and out of your dish!

TRACI'S EASY HASHBROWN CASSEROLE

MELISSA KNIGHT
ATHENS, AL

My dear friend Traci gave me this recipe after she brought these yummy potatoes to work. The casserole is so delicious we made at least 20 copies of the recipe to share!

1 c. onion, finely diced
1 t. seasoned salt
salt and pepper to taste
26-oz. can cream of chicken soup
1 c. butter, melted
4 c. shredded Cheddar cheese
30-oz. pkg. frozen shredded hashbrowns, partially thawed

In a bowl, mix together onion and seasonings. Stir in soup, butter and cheese; fold in hashbrowns. Transfer mixture to a greased 13"x9" baking pan. Bake, uncovered, at 350 degrees for 45 minutes, or until golden and bubbly.

Makes 8 to 10 servings.

SIMPLE DIRTY RICE FOR A CROWD

MICHELLE POWELL
VALLEY, AL

Easiest rice dish ever...delicious every time! Great for big get-togethers and potlucks.

Brown sausage and beef with onion in a large skillet over medium heat. Drain; set aside. Meanwhile, add water to a stockpot; bring to a boil over high heat. Stir in rice, celery and soup mixes. Reduce heat to medium-low. Simmer until rice is tender and water is nearly absorbed, stirring occasionally. Add sausage mixture and mushrooms with liquid. Season with salt and pepper. Divide mixture between 2 lightly greased 13"x9" glass baking pans. Top with water chestnuts. Bake, uncovered, at 350 degrees for 25 minutes.

Makes 15 servings.

2 lbs. ground pork sausage
1 lb. ground beef
1 c. onion, diced
9 c. water
2 c. long-cooking rice, uncooked
1 c. celery, chopped
3 2-1/4 oz. pkgs. noodle soup mix with chicken broth
8-oz. can sliced mushrooms
salt and pepper to taste
8-oz. can sliced water chestnuts, drained

LEMONY GARLIC ARTICHOKES

MICHELLE POWELL
VALLEY, AL

This is the easiest way I know to steam artichokes...and they are delicious! They make an impressive-looking side dish to serve when company is coming over.

3 to 4 artichokes
1/2 lemon
3 to 4 T. olive oil
salt to taste
4 cloves garlic, minced
1 c. chicken broth

Remove artichoke stems and slice one inch off the tops of artichokes. Rub lemon on cut sides of artichokes to prevent browning. Place artichokes in a slow cooker; drizzle juice from lemon and oil over artichokes. Season with salt; sprinkle with minced garlic. Pour broth around artichokes; add water until liquid is 2 inches deep. Cover and cook on high setting for about 3-1/2 hours, until artichoke hearts are tender. Serve artichokes drizzled with sauce from slow cooker.

Serves 3 to 4.

FIRE & ICE TOMATOES

MICHELLE MARBERRY
VALLEY, AL

Don't be fooled...this icy-cold salad is not spicy at all! It's perfect for potlucks or served over lettuce leaves at a luncheon.

5 tomatoes, cut into wedges
1 white onion, sliced and separated into rings
3/4 c. white vinegar
1/4 c. water
6 T. sugar
1 T. mustard seed
1/4 t. cayenne pepper
1 cucumber, peeled and sliced

Combine tomatoes and onion in a large bowl; set aside. In a small saucepan, combine vinegar, water, sugar and spices. Bring to a boil and cook for one minute, stirring until sugar dissolves. Pour over tomatoes and onion; gently toss to coat. Cover and refrigerate for at least 2 hours. Add cucumber; toss to coat. Refrigerate 8 hours to overnight before serving.

Makes 8 servings.

FRIED GREEN TOMATO CASSEROLE

DONNA CLEMENT
DAPHNE, AL

This is a delicious twist on fried green tomatoes that you will want to fix again & again. A friend from the Mississippi Gulf Coast taught me how to make it.

Combine all seasonings in a cup; set aside. In a lightly greased 13"x9" baking pan, layer half the tomatoes, half of seasoning mixture, half the onion and half the cheese. Repeat layers. Top with crackers; drizzle with melted butter. Bake, covered, at 400 degrees for 45 minutes; uncover and bake for 15 more minutes.

Makes 8 servings.

1/4 t. Cajun seasoning
1/4 t. garlic powder
1/4 t. lemon pepper seasoning
1 t. kosher salt
1/4 t. pepper
4 green tomatoes, thickly sliced
1 c. sweet onion, chopped
2 c. shredded Cheddar cheese
1 sleeve round buttery crackers, crushed
1/4 c. butter, melted

MASHED POTATO FILLING CASSEROLE

**MARY DONALDSON
ENTERPRISE, AL**

My dear friend Suzie is of Pennsylvania Dutch heritage. This is her mom's favorite potato recipe and a big part of her family's holiday gatherings. It has become one of my favorites too.

**4 c. soft bread cubes
1/2 c. butter, sliced
1/2 c. celery, chopped
2 T. onion, chopped
1/2 c. boiling water
3 eggs, beaten
2 c. milk
1-1/2 t. salt
1/2 t. pepper
2 c. mashed potatoes**

Place bread cubes in a heatproof bowl; set aside. Melt butter in a small saucepan over medium heat. Add celery and onion; cook until tender. Pour mixture over bread cubes; mix well. Add remaining ingredients; mix well after each addition. Mixture will be moist. Divide between 2 well greased one-quart casserole dishes. Bake, uncovered, at 350 degrees for 45 minutes.

Serves 8 to 10.

DINNERTIME CONVERSATION

Alabama was originally inhabited by Indigenous people. Today, traces of their occupancy, which spanned about 10,000 years, may be seen at Dust Cave, a Paleo-Indian site and at Russell Cave, a site dating to the Archaic period.

CORN CHIP SALAD TO GO

**MICHELLE POWELL
VALLEY, AL**

Perfect tailgate food! Just mix the salad and serve in individual corn chip bags.

In a large bowl, combine all ingredients except corn chips. Toss to mix; let stand for one hour. At serving time, slit open corn chip bags down one side. Spoon salad over corn chips in bags and serve immediately.

Serves 6.

1 to 2 ripe tomatoes, chopped

1 head iceberg lettuce, chopped

1 onion, chopped

16-oz. pkg. shredded Cheddar cheese

15-oz. can ranch-style beans, drained

8-oz. bottle Catalina salad dressing

6 2-oz. pkgs. corn chips

BACON-BROCCOLI SALAD

MICHELLE POWELL
VALLEY, AL

A hearty salad that everyone will love. Men really go for it!

10 slices bacon, crisply cooked and crumbled

2 bunches broccoli, finely chopped

3 3-1/4 oz. cans sliced black olives, drained

1 bunch green onions, finely chopped

1 c. mayonnaise

1/4 c. mayonnaise-style salad dressing

3/4 c. shredded Parmesan cheese

Italian salad dressing to taste

Combine bacon and vegetables in a large bowl; set aside. In a separate bowl, combine mayonnaise, mayonnaise-style salad dressing and Parmesan cheese. Spoon over vegetables; stir until all ingredients are moistened. Thin with Italian dressing as desired. Cover and refrigerate overnight.

Serves 12.

KITCHEN TIP

For easy chopped bacon, place uncooked bacon in the freezer for 10-15 minutes prior to cutting up, then chop and cook.

POTATO-LADY POTATOES

DIXIE BARKLEY
HOPE HULL, AL

When I brought these potatoes to a church supper, they were a big hit. A few days later, a lady came up to me in the grocery store. She was so excited and said, "Aren't you the potato lady?" I had to write the recipe down for her right there!

Place potatoes in a slow cooker. Combine all remaining ingredients; add to potatoes and mix well. Cover and cook on low setting for 2 to 3 hours, stirring occasionally.

Makes 12 to 15 servings.

4 15-oz. cans sliced potatoes, drained
2 10-3/4 oz. cans cream of celery soup
16-oz. container sour cream
1/2 lb. bacon, crisply cooked and crumbled
1 bunch green onions, sliced

NANA'S BAKED BEANS

EDNA CUMBEE WORTH
PHENIX CITY, AL

These are my famous baked beans I serve at every barbecue and lots of other occasions. My oldest daughter recently married...of course, my baked beans were served at the reception, much to everyone's delight!

In a deep skillet over medium heat, cook bacon until crisp; drain. Add remaining ingredients except pork & beans to bacon. Reduce heat to low; stir to mix. Add pork & beans to bacon mixture; mix well. Spoon bean mixture into a lightly greased 3-quart casserole dish. Bake, uncovered, at 350 degrees for about 30 minutes, until bubbly and heated through.

Serves 8.

1/2 lb. thick-sliced bacon, chopped
1 sweet onion, chopped
1 c. dark brown sugar, packed
1/3 c. molasses
1/4 c. Worcestershire sauce
1 T. mustard
3/4 c. catsup
2 15-oz. cans pork & beans, partially drained

CREAMED BAKED MUSHROOMS

MICHELLE POWELL
VALLEY, AL

This dish is scrumptious served over baked chicken, egg noodles or steamed rice.

1/3 c. butter, softened
1 T. fresh parsley, chopped
1-1/2 T. all-purpose flour
1 T. Dijon mustard
1 T. onion, grated
1 t. salt
1/8 t. cayenne pepper
1/8 t. nutmeg
1 lb. sliced mushrooms, divided
1 c. whipping cream

In a bowl, blend butter, parsley, flour, mustard, onion and seasonings; set aside. Layer half of mushrooms in a lightly greased 1-1/2 quart casserole dish; dot with half of butter mixture. Add another layer of mushrooms; dot with remaining butter. Pour cream over all. Bake, uncovered, at 375 degrees for 45 minutes, or until hot and bubbly.

Serves 4 to 6.

BESSIE'S HOT CORN

CHRISTY BONNER
BESSEMER, AL

One of my husband's great-aunts shared this recipe with me.

2 15-oz. cans corn, drained
2 8-oz. pkg's. cream cheese, cubed
3 to 4 jalapeño peppers, chopped
2 to 3 dashes hot pepper sauce
8-oz. pkg. shredded sharp Cheddar cheese, divided

Combine corn and cream cheese in a microwave-safe 2-quart casserole dish. Microwave, uncovered, on high setting for 5 minutes, stirring occasionally, until cream cheese and corn mix easily. Stir in jalapeños, hot sauce and one cup shredded cheese. Top with remaining shredded cheese. Microwave for an additional 3 minutes.

Serves 8.

ONION YORKSHIRE PUDDING

MELISSA KNIGHT
ATHENS, AL

This is the best side dish for any Christmas dinner! It goes well with just about any roast...beef, pork, chicken or ham.

In a cast-iron skillet over medium-high heat, sauté onion in butter until tender and golden. Add one teaspoon salt and pepper; spoon into an ungreased 9" pie plate. In a large bowl, combine flour and remaining salt. In a separate bowl, whisk together eggs, water and milk; add to flour mixture and whisk until just blended. Pour batter over onion mixture. Bake, uncovered, at 400 degrees for 30 to 35 minutes, until golden. Cut into wedges; serve warm.

1 onion, sliced
2 T. butter
2 t. salt, divided
1 t. pepper
3/4 c. plus
2 T. all-purpose flour
2 eggs, beaten
3/4 c. water
3/4 c. milk

Serves 6 to 8.

GRAM'S DRESSED-UP CARROTS

MARY DONALDSON
ENTERPRISE, AL

A childhood favorite for me! I would always ask my grandma to include this dish at Christmas and for all special meals when we gathered at her home.

In a saucepan, cover carrots with water; add salt and bring to a boil over high heat. Reduce heat to medium-low; cover and simmer for 10 to 12 minutes, until carrots are crisp-tender. Drain and set aside. In the same pan, combine remaining ingredients. Cook and stir over low heat until blended, about 3 minutes. Return carrots to pan; stir until glazed.

16-oz. pkg. baby carrots, sliced
1/2 t. salt
1/3 c. orange marmalade
2 T. butter
2 t. Dijon mustard
1/2 t. fresh ginger, peeled and grated

Makes 6 servings.

CHAPTER THREE

FOOTBALL STADIUM
Soups, Sandwiches & Breads

COZY UP WITH A BOWL OF HEARTY
SOUP AND WARM BREAD OR A TASTY
SANDWICH...PERFECT FOR GAME DAY OR
A COOL NIGHT ON THE FRONT PORCH IN
YOUR FAVORITE ROCKING CHAIR.

MOM'S CORN CHOWDER

MELISSA KNIGHT
ATHENS, AL

When I was in the third grade, my family and I lived in Louisville, Kentucky. One January morning, we awoke to find over 15 inches of unexpected snow on the ground! I still remember Mom making this delicious chowder with ingredients she had on hand...so cozy!

4 potatoes, peeled and
  cubed
1/8 t. salt
2 onions, diced
1/4 c. butter
2 14-3/4 oz. cans
  creamed corn
4 c. milk
5-oz. can evaporated
  milk
1/8 t. pepper

Cover potatoes with water in a large Dutch oven; add salt. Bring to a boil over medium-high heat; cook until nearly tender. Meanwhile, in a separate saucepan over medium heat, sauté onions in butter until tender. Add onion mixture to cooked potatoes; do not drain potatoes. Stir in remaining ingredients. Simmer over low heat for at least 30 minutes, stirring occasionally.

Serves 4 to 6.

DINNERTIME CONVERSATION

The 1991 movie Fried Green Tomatoes was inspired by the Irondale Café, 7 miles from downtown Birmingham, Alabama.

SLOW-COOKER CHICKEN CHILI

MARY JEFFERSON RABON MOBILE, AL

A game-day favorite! This has become known as our National Championship Soup. We have made it for the many championship games our Alabama Crimson Tide has played in....and won!

Place chicken in a 5-quart slow cooker. Add tomatoes with juice, corn with juice and beans. Top with salad dressing mix and seasonings; stir together. Place cream cheese on top. Cover and cook on low setting for 6 to 8 hours. Stir cream cheese into chili. Use 2 forks to shred chicken in slow cooker; stir together. Serve soup topped with Cheddar cheese, with tortilla chips on the side.

Makes 10 servings.

- 2 boneless, skinless chicken breasts
- 14-1/2 oz. can diced tomatoes with green chiles
- 15-1/4 oz. can corn
- 15-1/2 oz. can black beans, drained and rinsed
- 1-oz. pkg. ranch salad dressing mix
- 1 T. chili powder
- 1 t. ground cumin
- 1 t. onion powder
- 8-oz. pkg. light cream cheese, softened
- Garnish: shredded Cheddar cheese, tortilla chips

GRILLED BEEF & PEPPER SAMMIES

BETHANY SCOTT
HUNTSVILLE, AL

A countertop grill works well too...just place the filled loaf inside, close the lid and toast until golden.

12-inch loaf Italian
  bread, halved
  lengthwise
1/2 lb. deli roast beef,
  sliced
1/4 lb. provolone cheese,
  sliced
8-oz. jar roasted red
  peppers, drained and
  chopped
2 T. green olives with
  pimentos, diced
1 T. olive oil

Layer bottom half of loaf with roast beef, cheese, peppers and olives; add top of loaf. Brush oil lightly over both sides of loaf. Heat a large skillet over medium heat; add loaf carefully and cook for 2 to 3 minutes on each side, until golden and cheese has melted. Slice loaf into sections to serve.

Makes 4 to 6 sandwiches.

CHILI DOG SOUP

KATIE MARBERRY
VALLEY, AL

I created this recipe while in college, and it has now become a staple on my family's table. Customize this recipe by adding your family's personal favorite chili dog toppings. Kids love it! Serve with toasted hot dog buns or white bread.

15-oz. can chili
3 hot dogs, cut into thin
  rounds
3/4 c. pasteurized
  process cheese sauce
2 T. mustard
2 to 3 T. onion, diced

Combine chili, hot dogs and cheese sauce in a saucepan; simmer over medium heat for 10 minutes. Stir in mustard and onion. Continue cooking until hot dogs are heated through and soup is beginning to boil.

Serves 3.

HUG-IN-A-MUG SOUP

MICHELLE MARBERRY
VALLEY, AL

A quick-to-fix family favorite! Serve in big soup mugs with a hearty bread for a very comforting supper.

In a stockpot over medium heat, brown turkey; drain and set aside. In the same pot, melt butter over medium heat; sauté onion, garlic and green pepper until tender. Add remaining ingredients except pasta and bring to a boil. Stir in pasta. Simmer, uncovered, over medium heat for 10 minutes, or until pasta is tender.

Serves 8.

1 lb. ground turkey
1 T. butter
1 onion, chopped
3 cloves garlic, minced
1 green pepper, chopped
1. 35-oz. pkg. onion soup mix
16-oz. can navy beans, drained and rinsed
16-oz. can kidney beans, drained and rinsed
28-oz. can crushed tomatoes
28-oz. can diced tomatoes, drained
1 T. dried parsley
1 T. dried basil
8 c. water
salt and pepper to taste
1 c. small pasta shells, uncooked

ZESTY MINESTRONE

BETH HAGOPIAN
HUNTSVILLE, AL

This hearty soup reheats well and is the perfect addition to any lunchbox.

1 lb. Italian pork sausage links, sliced
2 t. oil
1 onion, chopped
1 green pepper, chopped
3 cloves garlic, chopped
28-oz. can whole tomatoes
2 potatoes, diced
1/4 c. fresh parsley, chopped
2 t. dried oregano
1 t. dried basil
1 t. fennel seed
1/2 t. red pepper flakes
salt and pepper to taste
4 c. beef broth
2 16-oz. cans kidney beans
1 c. elbow macaroni, uncooked

Sauté sausage in oil in a large saucepan over medium heat; drain. Add onion, green pepper and garlic; cook 5 minutes. Add tomatoes with juice, potatoes, seasonings and broth; bring to a boil. Reduce heat; simmer 30 minutes. Stir in undrained beans and macaroni; simmer an additional 10 minutes, or until macaroni is tender.

Makes 6 to 8 servings.

TURNIP GREEN SOUP

CHRISTY BONNER
BANKSTON, AL

This is a warming soup for a cold winter day. Mix up a pan of delicious cornbread and you have a hearty meal!

In a skillet over medium heat, brown sausage with onion and carrots. Transfer sausage mixture to a slow cooker; add greens, tomatoes with juice, peas and seasonings. Cover and cook on high setting for one to 2 hours.

Serves 6 to 8.

1 lb. mild or hot ground pork sausage

1 c. onion, chopped

1-1/2 c. carrots, peeled and chopped

27-oz. can seasoned turnip greens

14-oz. can seasoned turnip greens

10-oz. can diced tomatoes with green chiles

2 15-oz. cans black-eyed peas, drained and rinsed

1 t. red pepper flakes

1/2 t. pepper

DINNERTIME CONVERSATION

Alabama natives historically celebrate New Year's Day with good-luck foods like black-eyed peas, turnip or collard greens and cornbread

TACO CHILI WITH A TWIST

ANNETTE THOMAS
HUNTSVILLE, AL

My kids love eating this chili with tortilla chips or cornbread. You can use leftover taco beef from the night before or even make a big batch of beef and freeze half for later. I have used all sorts of canned beans, whatever I have on hand.

1 lb. ground beef

1-oz. pkg. taco seasoning mix

4 16-oz. cans assorted beans like Great Northern, pinto, kidney, chili and/or pork & beans

14-3/4 oz. can creamed corn

16-oz. bottle cocktail vegetable juice

Optional: shredded Cheddar cheese

Brown beef in a skillet over medium heat; drain. Stir in taco seasoning; transfer beef to a 6-quart slow cooker. Add beans, draining all except chili beans and pork & beans. Stir in corn. Add enough vegetable juice to fill slow cooker to within 2 inches of the top. Cover and cook on high setting for one to 2 hours, or on low setting for 3 to 4 hours, until heated through. Top with cheese, if desired.

Serves 8.

PRESENTATION

Easily win guests over with a soup buffet. Provide a couple different soups with a variety of toppings and breads to try!

SPICY MEXICAN CHICKEN SOUP

**JUDY WILSON
HUNTSVILLE, AL**

This soup uses basic ingredients that are slow-cooked to perfection. We like to serve it with Mexican-blend cheese sprinkled on top and tortilla chips. Feel free to add your own favorite toppings!

Place chicken in a 4 to 6-quart slow cooker. Add tomatoes with juice, chiles and corn. Pour in broth; add seasonings and stir gently. Cover and cook on low setting for 6 to 7 hours, until chicken is very tender. Remove chicken to a plate; cool and shred. Return shredded chicken to slow cooker and stir well. Add beans; cover and cook on low setting for another 30 minutes. Top with shredded cheese; serve with tortilla chips.

Makes 6 servings.

3 boneless, skinless chicken breasts

2 14-1/2 oz. cans petite diced tomatoes

4-oz. can chopped green chiles

2 c. frozen corn

14-1/2 oz. can reduced-sodium chicken broth

2 T. chili powder

1 T. ground cumin

1/2 t. salt

1/4 t. cayenne pepper, or to taste

15-oz. can black beans, drained and rinsed

Garnish: shredded Mexican-blend cheese, tortilla chips

AUTUMN CHILI SOUP

DEBRA COLLINS
GAYLESVILLE, AL

This is one of my family's favorite chili dishes during football season.
Serve with corn chips.

1 lb. ground beef

14-1/2 oz. can can diced tomatoes

15-1/2 oz. can kidney beans, drained and rinsed

15-oz. can corn, drained

10-oz. can diced tomatoes and green chiles, drained

2 c. water

1-oz. pkg. taco seasoning mix

Brown beef in a large stockpot over medium heat; drain. Stir in undrained tomatoes and remaining ingredients; bring to a boil. Reduce heat to low. Simmer, uncovered, for 15 to 20 minutes, stirring occasionally.

Makes 6 servings.

ROSE'S CREAM
OF POTATO SOUP

ROSE CANNON
GORDON, AL

Garnish this thick, cheesy soup with snipped chives.

In a large saucepan over medium heat, sauté onion in butter. Add potatoes and enough water to cover; stir in seasonings. Cook until potatoes break apart with a fork. Stir in soup; add cheeses and stir until melted. Stir in milk to desired thickness; adjust seasoning. Cook, stirring occasionally, for a few more minutes until thickened.

Makes 4 to 6 servings.

1/2 onion, chopped

1/4 c. butter

8 potatoes, peeled and cubed

2 t. roasted garlic & red bell pepper seasoning blend

salt and pepper to taste

10-3/4 oz. can cream of chicken soup

1 c. shredded mozzarella cheese

1 c. shredded Parmesan cheese

1/2 c. Colby cheese, shredded

2 to 2-1/2 c. milk

CHICKEN GUMBO

ANNA OGLE
SYLACAUGA, AL

You'll really enjoy this flavorful soup...it will warm you up on a chilly day!

3 1/2-lb. boneless, skinless chicken breasts
4 c. water
1/3 c. onion, chopped
16-oz. can tomatoes
1/3 c. rice, uncooked
salt to taste
2 1/2 t. pepper
3 to 4 c. okra, chopped
1-1/2 c. corn
1/2 t. dried basil
1/4 t. garlic salt

Place chicken and 4 cups water in a Dutch oven. Cover and bring to a boil; reduce heat and simmer one hour, or until chicken is tender and juices run clear when chicken is pierced. Remove chicken from Dutch oven and set aside; when chicken is cool enough to handle, cut into bite-size pieces and refrigerate until ready to use. Chill broth several hours; skim off and discard any fat from top. Stir onion, tomatoes, rice, salt and pepper into broth in Dutch oven. Bring to a boil and simmer 30 minutes. Add chicken and remaining ingredients. Continue to simmer an additional 30 minutes.

Serves 7 to 8.

CURE-ALL CHICKEN SOUP

MICHELLE POWELL
VALLEY, AL

This simple soup clears your sniffles and soothes your heart as it tickles your tastebuds!

4 chicken breasts
12 c. water
2 15-oz. cans diced tomatoes with green chiles
2 10-oz. pkgs. frozen creamed corn, thawed
1 c. milk
salt and pepper to taste

In a stockpot, combine chicken and water. Simmer over medium-low heat until chicken is tender. Remove chicken to a plate, reserving broth in pot. Add tomatoes with juice and corn to reserved broth. Dice chicken and add to broth, discarding skin and bones. Simmer over low heat for 2 hours. Stir in milk without boiling; season with salt and pepper.

Makes 10 servings.

ANNETTE'S CHILI SOUP

ANNETTE CERAVOLO
HOOVER, AL

This soup has been made by family & friends over the years. Each person has added something to it...this is my version. It's spicy and so good. Serve with biscuits or cornbread.

In a skillet over medium heat, brown beef and onion together; drain well. Combine beef mixture, undrained beans, undrained tomatoes and remaining ingredients in a large slow cooker. Cover and cook on high setting for 3 to 4 hours.

Serves 4.

1 lb. lean ground beef
1 onion, finely chopped
3 to 4 15-1/2 oz. cans kidney beans
10-oz. can diced tomatoes with chiles
1/2 c. dry red wine or beef broth
4 t. chili powder
1/2 t. garlic, minced
salt and pepper to taste

LEMONY CHICKEN SOUP

ANNETTE CERAVOLO
HOOVER, AL

This is good with or without spinach and it's quick to make.

Heat oil in large saucepan over medium-high heat; add chicken and onion. Cook, stirring occasionally, about 5 minutes, until chicken is no longer pink. Add chicken broth; bring to a boil. Stir in pasta. Cook for 5 to 7 minutes, until pasta is tender. Stir in spinach, if using, and lemon juice. Season with salt and pepper. Heat through.

Serves 4.

1 T. olive oil
1 lb. boneless, skinless chicken breasts, cubed
1 onion, diced
4 c. chicken broth, or more if needed
1 c. small star pasta, uncooked
Optional: 6-oz. pkg. baby spinach
2 T. lemon juice
salt and pepper to taste

COMFORT CHILI

MELISSA KNIGHT
ELKMONT, AL

I can remember coming into the house after playing in the snow. My mom would have a huge pot of this chili simmering on the stove. Our family always eats chili with peanut butter sandwiches...try it, please, it is delicious!

3 lbs. ground beef chuck
1 lb. hot ground pork sausage
3 onions, chopped
2 T. garlic, minced
2 T. all-purpose flour
1 T. sugar
1-1/4 oz. pkg. chili seasoning mix
1 t. dried oregano
1 t. salt
2 28-oz. cans whole tomatoes
3 16-oz. cans kidney beans, drained

Combine beef, sausage, onions and garlic in a large soup pot. Cover and cook over medium heat until beef and sausage are no longer pink. Drain; sprinkle with flour, sugar, seasoning mix and seasonings, stirring well. Reduce heat to medium-low. Cover and simmer for one hour, stirring occasionally. Stir in tomatoes with juice and beans; simmer for 20 more minutes.

Makes 12 servings.

BRUNSWICK STEW

CHRISTY BONNER
BESSEMER, AL

I love Brunswick stew! After much trial & error, I've found the right combination suited to my taste. This is a true crowd-pleaser and always keeps 'em coming back for more. One Christmas with my grandmother's family, everyone scraped the pot clean! They all left with a copy of this recipe in hand, they loved it so much.

Place pork roast fat-side up in a 6-quart slow cooker. Season well with salt and pepper. Cover and cook on low setting for 8 to 10 hours, until very tender. Drain and cool; shred with 2 forks. This step may be done a day ahead. Next, in a large stockpot, combine chicken and water. Bring to a boil over medium-high heat. Reduce heat to low; cover and simmer for 35 to 40 minutes. Remove chicken to a plate and cool, reserving broth in stockpot. Cut chicken into bite-size pieces, discarding bones and skin; set aside. Add potatoes and onion to reserved broth. Bring to a boil; reduce heat and cook until vegetables are tender, about 25 minutes. Stir in pork, chicken, tomatoes with juice and remaining ingredients. Simmer, uncovered, over low heat for one hour, stirring occasionally.

Makes 15 servings.

4-lb. Boston butt pork roast
salt and pepper to taste
4 chicken breasts
10 c. water
3 potatoes, peeled and chopped
1 onion, chopped
28-oz. can diced tomatoes
26-oz. bottle catsup
2 15-1/4 oz. cans corn, drained
2 14-3/4 oz. cans creamed corn
1/2 c. Worcestershire sauce
1/4 c. butter
2 T. smoke-flavored cooking sauce
2 t. hot pepper sauce, or to taste

MOMMA'S MEXICAN STEW

MICHELLE POWELL
VALLEY, AL

Not a soup, not a chili! This hearty stew comes together quick and tastes
even better served the next day. Excellent with cornbread.

4 t. oil
1-1/2 lbs. stew beef cubes
1 c. onion, chopped
1 to 2 cloves garlic,
  minced
2 T. chili powder
14-1/2 oz. can diced
  tomatoes
16-oz. pkg. frozen corn,
  thawed
2 c. water
1 t. salt
1/4 t. pepper

Heat oil in a large skillet over medium heat. Add beef; brown on all sides. Add onion and garlic; cook until onion is translucent. Add chili powder; stir to coat beef. Add tomatoes with juice and remaining ingredients. Reduce heat to medium-low. Cover and simmer for one hour, or until beef is tender, stirring occasionally.

Makes 6 servings.

GRANNY'S JALAPEÑO CORNBREAD

TIFFANY JOHNSON
GRANT, AL

No bowl of soup or chili is complete without cornbread! This recipe is
delicious and easy to make.

1-1/4 c. cornmeal
1/2 t. baking soda
1/2 t. salt
2/3 c. buttermilk
1/3 c. oil
2 eggs, beaten
1 c. creamed corn
1 c. shredded Cheddar
  cheese
1 to 2 T. jalapeño
  peppers, chopped

In a bowl, mix cornmeal, baking soda and salt. In a separate bowl, mix buttermilk, oil and eggs. Stir into cornmeal mixture until most lumps are dissolved; don't overmix. Stir in remaining ingredients. Pour batter into a greased 13"x9" baking pan. Bake at 375 degrees for 30 to 40 minutes. Cut into squares.

Makes 15 servings.

EL PASO SOUP

**CAROLYN BRITTON
MILLRY, AL**

Quick & easy, this recipe is a great hit with children and adults. Perfect for a ballgame treat!

Brown turkey and onion in a skillet over medium heat; drain. Combine turkey mixture, tomatoes with juice and remaining ingredients except garnish in a 6-quart slow cooker. Cover and cook on low setting for 2 to 3 hours. If mixture is too thick, stir in a little extra broth or water. Serve topped with shredded cheese and tortilla chips.

Serves 12 to 15.

2 lbs. ground turkey

3/4 c. onion, chopped

14-1/2 oz. can diced tomatoes

10-oz. can diced tomatoes with green chiles

2 11-oz. cans white shoepeg corn

15-1/2 oz. can red kidney beans

15-1/2 oz. can pinto beans

15-1/2 oz. can black beans

2 1-1/4 oz. pkgs. taco seasoning mix

2 1-oz. pkgs. ranch salad dressing mix

Garnish: shredded Cheddar cheese, tortilla chips

EASY ITALIAN STEW

MICHELLE POWELL
VALLEY, AL

*Frozen vegetables, canned tomatoes and flavorful herbs make this
a quick-prep slow-cooked meal that is hearty, hot and delicious!*

1 T. oil
1 lb. boneless beef round
   steak, cubed
14-1/2 oz. can diced
   tomatoes with basil,
   garlic & oregano
1/2 lb. redskin potatoes,
   quartered
4 c. water
14-oz. can beef broth
1-1/2 c. onion, chopped
2 carrots, peeled and
   sliced
1 zucchini, sliced
1 c. dried Great
   Northern beans
1/2 c. pearled barley,
   uncooked
4 cloves garlic, minced
1-1/2 t. dried rosemary
1 t. dried sage
1-1/2 t. salt
1 t. pepper
1 c. fresh baby spinach
Garnish: grated
   Parmesan cheese

Heat oil in a skillet over medium heat. Brown beef in oil; drain. Combine beef, tomatoes with juice and remaining ingredients except spinach and garnish in a slow cooker. Cover and cook on high setting for 6 hours, or until beef, vegetables and beans are tender. Stir in spinach; cover and cook for an additional 20 minutes. Ladle soup into bowls; sprinkle with Parmesan cheese.

Serves 8 to 10.

NANA'S POTATO SOUP

CHRISTY BONNER
BERRY, AL

*Handed down in my family for many generations, this recipe can
always be found at our winter church socials. It's true comfort food for
a chilly evening.*

Melt margarine in a Dutch oven over medium heat.
Stir in flour one tablespoon at a time until smooth.
Add broth, chives and parsley; stir until thickened.
Add half-and-half, stirring until well mixed. Stir in
potatoes and heat through; sprinkle to taste with salt
and pepper. Garnish as desired.

Makes 6 to 8 servings.

1/2 c. margarine

10 T. all-purpose flour

4 14-1/2 oz. cans chicken
broth

1 T. fresh chives,
chopped

1 T. fresh parsley,
chopped

4 c. half-and-half

6 to 8 potatoes, peeled,
cubed and cooked

salt and pepper to taste

Garnish: shredded
Cheddar cheese, bacon
bits, chopped green
onions

MINI CHEDDAR LOAVES

MARY KING
ASHVILLE, AL

*Mother and I have enjoyed this simple recipe for many years...it's great to
take to parties and potlucks.*

Combine cheese and biscuit mix in a large bowl. In
a separate bowl, beat together eggs and milk; stir
into cheese mixture. Pour into 2 greased 7"x4" loaf
pans. Bake at 350 degrees for 40 to 55 minutes.
Check for doneness after 40 minutes by inserting a
toothpick near center. If not done, bake an additional
5 minutes and test again. Repeat until done.

Makes 2 mini loaves.

2-1/2 c. shredded
Cheddar cheese

2 eggs, beaten

1-1/4 c. milk

3-1/2 c. biscuit baking
mix

GRANDMOTHER'S CHICKEN NOODLE SOUP

**MARY KING
ASHVILLE, AL**

Grandmother used to make this soup whenever anyone was sick. She said it was made with chicken and noodles and lots of love...that was the secret ingredient. She also said that this is the easiest soup to make right out of the pantry. Now it is time to get a bowl and help yourself to a great soup.

2 to 3 boneless, skinless chicken breasts

4 c. water

15-oz. can sweet peas, drained

2 14-1/2 oz. cans sliced carrots, drained

1/4 c. butter

1 t. garlic powder

salt and pepper to taste

12-oz. pkg. medium egg noodles, uncooked

Optional: 1 to 2 14-oz. cans chicken broth

In a soup pot, combine chicken and water. Bring to a boil over medium- high heat. Cook for 35 to 45 minutes, until chicken is cooked through. Remove chicken to a plate to cool, reserving broth in soup pot. Add peas, carrots, butter and seasonings to reserved broth. Cut chicken into bite-size pieces and add to broth. Bring back to a boil and add desired amount of noodles; cook until noodles are soft. If more broth is desired, add optional broth, one can at a time, to desired consistency; warm through.

Makes 6 to 8 servings.

OLD-TIMER BEEF STEW

BEN GOTHARD
JEMISON, AL

This dish is just right with a hot grilled cheese sandwich or crisp cornbread. Spoon into a thermos for cool-weather outings such as football games or hayrides. It even freezes well and tastes good reheated. You can even enjoy a slow-cooker version of this soup... simply cook on the low setting for 6 hours, then add the flour to thicken as instructed. Enjoy!

Place beef, margarine, garlic salt, pepper, vegetables, catsup and 12 cups water in a large stockpot; bring to a boil. Reduce heat and simmer, covered, 35 to 45 minutes or until beef is tender. Whisk flour and remaining water in a bowl. When vegetables are tender, carefully remove 2 cups of hot broth and whisk into the flour mixture to thicken; stir until smooth and return to stockpot. Simmer 10 minutes.

Makes 12 servings.

2 lbs. stew beef, cubed
1/2 c. margarine
1 T. garlic salt
1 T. pepper
2 lbs. potatoes, cubed
4 carrots, peeled and sliced
1 to 2 onions, chopped
4 stalks celery, chopped
1 c. frozen green peas
1 c. frozen corn
2 14-1/2 oz. cans diced tomatoes
1-1/2 c. catsup
12-1/2 c. water, divided
1/2 c. all-purpose flour

MEXICAN CORNBREAD MUFFINS

**BECKY FOSTER
MONROEVILLE, AL**

*Best Mexican cornbread I have ever tasted! I have had this recipe for
30 years. If you don't have buttermilk on hand, just use milk for all of it.*

3 eggs
3/4 c. buttermilk
3/4 c. milk
1 T. sugar
1 t. salt
1/2 t. pepper
2 c. self-rising cornmeal
1 c.oil
12-oz. can sweet corn &
  diced peppers, drained
2 jalapeño peppers,
  chopped
3/4 c. onion, chopped
1/2 c. shredded Cheddar
  cheese

Beat eggs in a large bowl. Add remaining
ingredients; mix well. Spoon batter into greased
muffin cups, filling 2/3 full. Bake at 400 degrees for
20 to 30 minutes.

Makes 2 dozen.

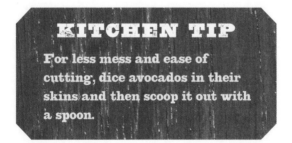

KITCHEN TIP

For less mess and ease of
cutting, dice avocados in their
skins and then scoop it out with
a spoon.

MAMA'S SOUTHERN HUSHPUPPIES

CORA PHILLIPS
OZARK, AL

This recipe was handed down from my mama...it's the only one she ever used. These are a yummy side served with fried catfish!

In a large bowl, combine cornmeal, flour, sugar, salt and baking powder. Add remaining ingredients except oil. Mixture will be thick but should not be dry. If dry, add a little more buttermilk. Heat a deep fryer of peanut oil to 350 degrees. Carefully drop batter from a small spoon. Fry in small batches until dark golden on all sides. Drain on paper towels.

Serves 8 to 10.

1 c. white cornmeal

1/2 c. all-purpose flour

1-1/2 to 2 T. sugar

1 t. salt

2 T. baking powder

3/4 c. buttermilk

1 egg, beaten

1 onion, chopped

Optional: 1 jalapeño
    pepper, chopped and
    seeds removed

peanut oil for frying

QUICK BEAN & BACON SOUP

MICHELLE POWELL
VALLEY, AL

The kids love this soup, and I can serve it up in 30 minutes. Use kitchen shears to make dicing the bacon a breeze.

In a soup pot over medium heat, cook bacon until crisp. Drain most of the drippings; set aside bacon on a paper towel-lined plate. In remaining drippings, sauté onion, celery and garlic until tender. Stir in tomatoes, beans and broth; bring to a boil. Reduce heat to low; simmer, uncovered, for 15 minutes. Stir in bacon just before serving.

Makes 6 servings.

1/2 lb. bacon, diced

1 onion, diced

1 stalk celery, diced

2 cloves garlic, minced

14-1/2 oz. can diced
    tomatoes, drained

2 15-oz. cans pork &
    beans

2 14-1/2 oz. cans beef
    broth

HOMEMADE CHICKEN–TOMATO STEW

LINDA HILL
ATHENS, AL

This stew is good any time of the year.

- **3 to 4 boneless, skinless chicken breasts**
- **5 c. water**
- **2 15-oz. cans corn**
- **28-oz. can diced tomatoes**
- **2 T. chicken bouillon granules**
- **1 onion, diced**
- **2 potatoes, peeled and diced**
- **10-3/4 oz. can tomato soup**
- **2 T. hickory smoke-flavored cooking sauce**
- **salt and pepper to taste**

Combine chicken and water in a soup pot. Simmer over medium heat until chicken is tender. Remove chicken with a slotted spoon, reserving broth. Shred chicken and return to broth. Add remaining ingredients except salt and pepper; stir well. Simmer over low heat for 45 minutes. Add salt and pepper to taste.

Serves 6 to 8.

DILLY CHICKEN SANDWICHES

REBECCA BILLINGTON
BIRMINGHAM, AL

This is a great sandwich to make for a family get-together. We always add several bread & butter pickles to our sandwiches... we think they make the sandwich taste even better!

Place one chicken breast between 2 pieces of wax paper. Using a mallet, flatten to 1/4-inch thickness. Repeat with remaining chicken; set aside. In a skillet over medium-high heat, melt 3 tablespoons butter; stir in garlic and 1/2 teaspoon dill weed. Add chicken; cook on both sides until juices run clear. Remove and keep warm. Spread both sides of bread with remaining butter. In a skillet or griddle, grill bread on both sides until golden. Combine remaining ingredients except garnish, and spread on one side of 4 slices grilled bread. Top with chicken; garnish as desired. Top with remaining bread.

Makes 4.

- 4 boneless, skinless chicken breasts
- 6 T. butter, softened and divided
- 1 clove garlic, minced
- 3/4 t. dill weed, divided
- 8 slices French bread
- 4 T. cream cheese, softened
- 2 t. lemon juice
- Garnish: lettuce leaves, tomato slices, bread & butter pickles

DINNERTIME CONVERSATION

In the winter of 1903, an Alabama woman watched how the streetcar motorman had to leave the vehicle and wipe the snow and sleet from the windshield. As a solution, she came up with the idea for a swinging arm device with a rubber blade that the driver could use inside the vehicle. Thus windshield wipers were born!

CHAPTER FOUR

CHEAHA MOUNTAIN

Mains

FILL THEM UP WITH A STICK-TO-THE-RIBS MEAL THAT IS FULL OF FLAVOR AND HEARTY ENOUGH TO SATISFY EVEN THE BIGGEST APPETITE.

SCALLOPED POTATOES & HAM

MICHELLE POWELL
VALLEY, AL

Good old-fashioned comfort food! Using unpeeled potatoes, ham from the deli and pre-shredded cheese gets this dish into the oven in no time at all.

6 potatoes, sliced 3/8-inch thick

1 onion, thinly sliced and separated into rings

1-1/2 c. cooked ham, cut into small cubes

3/4 c. shredded mozzarella cheese

3/4 c. shredded Cheddar cheese

3/4 c. shredded Colby Jack cheese

6 T. all-purpose flour

1/4 c. butter, cut into small cubes

salt and pepper to taste

2 c. milk

5-oz. can evaporated milk

In a greased deep 13"x9" baking pan, layer potatoes, onion, ham and cheeses, making 2 or 3 layers. Sprinkle each layer with flour, dot with butter and season with salt and pepper. Combine milks; pour over layers. Season with more salt and pepper. Bake, uncovered, at 325 degrees for one hour, or until potatoes are fork-tender.

Makes 6 servings.

CHICKEN CASHEW CASSEROLE

ANNETTE CERAVOLO
HOOVER, AL

My neighbor made this dish for us when my daughter was born, 30 years ago. I've added my own touches over the years and my family loves it. I like to serve it with a tossed salad and steamed veggies.

In a large bowl, combine all ingredients, reserving half of the noodles. Mix lightly and spoon into a greased 2-quart casserole dish. Sprinkle reserved noodles on top. Bake, uncovered, at 325 degrees for 30 minutes, or until hot and bubbly.

Makes 4 servings.

1 c. cooked chicken, diced

10-3/4 oz. can cream of mushroom or celery soup

1 c. celery, diced

1/2 c. onion, diced

1/2 c. chopped cashews

1/4 c. chicken broth

salt and pepper to taste

3-oz. can chow mein noodles, divided

PRESENTATION

Add a fabric bow around the bottom of cake stands, stemmed glasswear or serving utensils for a pop of color.

SOUTHERN PORK NACHOS

BETHANY SCOTT
HUNTSVILLE, AL

Try these instead of ground beef nachos.

2 15-oz. cans pinto
  beans, drained and
  rinsed
4 c. water
4-oz. can chopped green
  chiles
2 T. chili powder
2 t. ground cumin
1 t. dried oregano
salt and pepper to taste
4-lb. pork shoulder roast
16-oz. pkg. tortilla chips
Garnish: shredded
  Mexican-blend cheese,
  sour cream, salsa,
  sliced black olives,
  sliced jalapeño peppers

Combine beans, water, chiles and spices in a large slow cooker; mix well. Add roast; cover and cook on low setting for 4 hours. Remove roast and shred, discarding any bones; return pork to slow cooker. Cover and cook on low setting for an additional 2 to 4 hours, adding more water if necessary. To serve, arrange tortilla chips on serving plates. Spoon pork mixture over chips; garnish as desired.

Makes 8 to 10 servings.

CHILI RELLENO CASSEROLE

MICHELLE POWELL
VALLEY, AL

This makes a great easy side dish on a Mexican buffet or taco night!

27-oz. can green chile
  pepper strips, drained
  and divided
32-oz. pkg. shredded
  Cheddar Jack cheese,
  divided
4 eggs, beaten
1 c. milk
3 T. biscuit baking mix

In a greased 13"x9" baking pan, layer half each of chiles and cheese; repeat layers and set aside. In a bowl, whisk eggs with milk. Stir in baking mix and pour over top. Bake, uncovered, at 350 degrees for 40 minutes, or until bubbly and golden.

Makes 8 servings.

Best-Ever Lemon Bars, p132

Whether you are looking for a quick breakfast to start the day off right, no-fuss party fare for those special guests, satisfying soups and sandwiches for the perfect lunch, main dishes to bring them to the table fast, or a sweet little something to savor at the end of the meal, you'll love these recipes from the amazing cooks in beautiful **Alabama**.

Turnip Green Soup, p57

Johnny Appleseed Toast, p9

Scalloped Sweet Potatoes & Apples, p32

Chocolatey Cocoa Gravy, p136

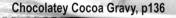

Comforting Creamed Corn, p36

Berry-Rhubarb Pie, p130

Grilled Beef & Pepper Sammies, p54

Easy Spaghetti & Meatballs, p90

lled Chicken with White BBQ Sauce, p88

y Chicken Sandwiches, p75

Mexican Roasted Cauliflower, p31

Cinnamon-Ginger Toasted Pecan Waffles, p

Sausage Muffins, p8

Pineapple Pudding, p131

Italian Fried Green Tomatoes, p114

Granny's Jalapeño Cornbread, p66

Zesty Minestrone, p56

Southern Pork Nachos, p80

Deep-Fried Pimento Cheese & Celery Bites, p122

Hug-in-a-Mug Soup, p55

Pumpkin Bars with Cream Cheese Icing, p144

Parmesan Baked Chicken, p87

PARMESAN BAKED CHICKEN

GINA POWELL
GADSDEN, AL

I tried this hand-me-down recipe when I was looking for something different to make with chicken. The bottom of the chicken will be more browned than the top.

In a bowl, combine butter and garlic. In another bowl, combine bread crumbs, Parmesan cheese and seasonings. Dip chicken in butter mixture to coat; dredge in bread crumb mixture. Place chicken into an ungreased 13"x9" baking pan. Drizzle remaining butter mixture over chicken. Bake, uncovered, at 400 degrees for 20 to 25 minutes, until juices run clear when pierced.

Makes 4 to 6 servings.

1/2 c. butter, melted

1 clove garlic, minced

1 c. Italian-flavored dry bread crumbs

1/3 c. grated Parmesan cheese

2 T. fresh parsley

1/4 t. salt

1/4 t. garlic powder

pepper to taste

Optional: 1/2 t. Italian seasoning

4 to 6 boneless, skinless chicken breasts

JUST FOR FUN

The Vulcan statue, the icon of Birmingham, Alabama, is the largest cast iron statue in the world. The 56-foot tall statue (from toe to spear point) depicts the Roman god Vulcan, and is the world's largest iron-ore statue. It weighs 120,000 pounds and was was designed by the Italian artist Giuseppe Moretti.

GRILLED CHICKEN WITH WHITE BBQ SAUCE

BETHANY SCOTT
HUNTSVILLE, AL

Grilled chicken with a spicy rub and a creamy sauce...you're going to love it! Be sure to allow enough time for the chicken to marinate.

**3 lbs. chicken thighs
and drumsticks**
1 T. dried thyme
1 T. dried oregano
1 T. ground cumin
1 T. paprika
1 t. onion powder
1 t. salt
1/2 t. pepper

Pat chicken dry with paper towels; set aside. Combine seasonings in a bowl; rub mixture evenly over chicken. Place chicken in a large plastic zipping bag. Seal and chill 4 hours. Make White BBQ Sauce at least 2 hours ahead of serving time; refrigerate. Shortly before serving time, remove chicken from bag, discarding bag. Grill chicken, covered, over medium-high heat for 8 to 10 minutes per side, until crisp, golden and chicken juices run clear when pierced. Serve chicken with sauce.

Serves 4 to 6.

White BBQ Sauce:

Stir together all ingredients. Cover and refrigerate for at least 2 hours.

WHITE BBQ SAUCE:
1-1/2 c. mayonnaise
**1/4 c. white wine
vinegar**
1 clove garlic, minced
**1 T. spicy brown
mustard**
**2 t. prepared
horseradish**
1 t. sugar
1/2 t. salt
1 T. pepper

VEGGIE SPAGHETTI PIE

MARY DONALDSON
ENTERPRISE, AL

To please my vegetarian guests, I made my favorite spaghetti pie minus the pepperoni slices I usually include. My guests loved it and asked for the recipe.

Cook spaghetti according to package directions, just until tender; drain. Stir in 2 tablespoons butter, egg and 1/2 cup Parmesan cheese. Press mixture into a 10" pie plate coated with non-stick vegetable spray. Spread cottage cheese over spaghetti mixture; set aside. In a skillet over medium heat, cook onion and yellow pepper in remaining butter until soft. Add artichokes and mushrooms; mix well. Spoon vegetable mixture over cottage cheese; top with remaining Parmesan cheese. Bake, uncovered, at 350 degrees for 25 to 30 minutes, until golden and heated through. Let stand 5 minutes before cutting.

Makes 6 to 8 servings.

- 7-oz. pkg. spaghetti, uncooked
- 3 T. butter, softened and divided
- 1 egg, beaten
- 1 c. grated Parmesan cheese, divided
- 1/2 c. small-curd cottage cheese
- 1 onion, chopped
- 1 yellow pepper, chopped
- 6-oz. jar artichoke hearts, drained and chopped
- 4-oz. can sliced portabella mushrooms, drained

KITCHEN TIP

Place a damp paper towel or two under your cutting board to keep it from moving around while you slice and dice.

EASY SPAGHETTI & MEATBALLS

STEPHANIE WISENHUNT
BIRMINGHAM, AL

One taste of this homemade sauce, and family & friends will think that it has simmered all day long. You don't have to share that it only took 20 minutes to make!

10-oz. pkg. spaghetti, uncooked

24 frozen, cooked Italian-style meatballs, thawed

2 14-oz. cans Italian-style diced tomatoes

2 6-oz. cans tomato paste

1/2 c. water

2 t. Italian seasoning

2 t. sugar

Optional: grated Parmesan cheese

Cook pasta according to package directions; keep pasta warm. Meanwhile, add meatballs, undrained tomatoes and next 4 ingredients to a Dutch oven. Cook over medium heat 20 minutes, stirring occasionally. Serve over hot cooked pasta. Sprinkle with Parmesan cheese, if desired.

Serves 4 to 6.

PRESENTATION

For a pretty presentation, serve potato, pasta or fruit salads on top of a leaf of Romaine lettuce.

ONE-DISH STEAK SUPPER

MICHELLE POWELL
VALLEY, AL

Steak and potatoes...quick & easy hearty comfort food.

Season steak on all sides with salt and pepper. Arrange in a lightly greased 13"x9" baking pan. Dot with butter; drizzle Worcestershire sauce over steak. Arrange vegetables on top. Cover with heavy aluminum foil. Bake at 350 degrees for 1-1/4 hours. Remove foil; bake another 15 minutes, or until steak is browned

Makes 6 servings.

- 1-1/2 lbs. beef top round steak, cut into serving-size pieces
- salt and pepper to taste
- 4 T. butter, sliced
- 4 T. Worcestershire sauce
- 4 potatoes, peeled and thickly sliced
- 1 onion, sliced and separated into rings
- 5 carrots, peeled and sliced
- 1 green pepper, cut into rings

DELICIOUS COLA ROAST

MICHELLE POWELL
VALLEY, AL

Easiest roast ever...and it turns out perfect every time! Makes great barbecue-like sandwiches. Great to make ahead because it tastes even better the second day. A tailgating favorite!

With a sharp knife, score roast in several places. Fill each slit with salt, pepper and garlic powder. Heat oil in a Dutch oven over medium-high heat. Add roast and brown on all sides. Pour cola and sauces over roast. Cover and bake at 325 degrees for 3 hours, or until very tender. Spoon onto buns.

Makes 16 servings.

- 4-lb. beef chuck or rump roast
- garlic powder, salt and pepper to taste
- 3 T. oil
- 1-1/2 c. cola
- 12-oz. bottle chili sauce
- 1/4 c. Worcestershire sauce
- 3 T. hot pepper sauce, or to taste
- 16 sandwich buns, split

SASSY SAUSAGE JAMBALAYA

DEBRA ELLIOTT
BIRMINGHAM, AL

This quick & easy dish is a family favorite. I've added a few fresh vegetables to get my grandson Nicholas to eat his veggies.

3 T. butter
1 green pepper, diced
1 yellow pepper, diced
1 red pepper, diced
1 sweet onion, diced
1 to 2 tomatoes, diced
1 lb. smoked pork
    sausage, sliced into
    1-inch rounds
8-1/2 oz. pkg.
    microwaveable Cajun
    rice & red beans

Add butter to a large skillet; melt over medium heat. Sauté peppers, onion and tomatoes for one to 2 minutes. Add sausage to skillet; heat through. Meanwhile, prepare rice in microwave according to package directions. Stir one cup cooked rice into mixture in skillet; reserve remaining rice for another meal. Simmer for 3 to 5 minutes to allow flavors to blend.

Serves 4.

CHEESY HASHBROWNS & BEEF

AMANDA GLADDEN
ONEONTA, AL

A favorite comfort-food meal for my kids and myself.

1 lb. ground beef
1/2 c. onion, chopped
1/2 c. green pepper,
    chopped
2 T. oil
2 to 3 potatoes, peeled
    and diced
seasoned salt to taste
10-oz. can diced
    tomatoes with green
    chiles
1 c. shredded Cheddar
    cheese

In a large skillet over medium heat, combine beef, onion and green pepper. Cook until beef is browned and onion is tender; drain. Meanwhile, heat oil in a separate skillet. Cook potatoes until tender and golden; season with salt. Add potatoes and tomatoes with juice to beef mixture. Cook for 5 to 10 minutes, stirring occasionally. Remove from heat; top with cheese. Cover and let stand until cheese melts, about 5 minutes.

Makes 4 servings.

MIMI'S SPAGHETTI & CHICKEN

JANICE FRY
HOOVER, AL

My mother gave me this versatile recipe when my five children were small, saying I would have most of the ingredients in my pantry. As a busy mom, I used this recipe almost every week because it was easy, the kids loved it and, most of all, it was cheap! Now, my children are grown and married with children and guess what? This recipe continues on in each of their kitchens! It's a life-saver!

Cook pasta according to package directions, just until tender; drain. Meanwhile, mix together remaining ingredients except cheese and French fried onions; set aside. Transfer pasta to a greased 13"x9" baking pan; add chicken mixture and stir gently. Top with cheese. Bake, uncovered, at 350 degrees for 20 to 30 minutes, until bubbly and cheese has melted. Top with onions during the last 5 to 7 minutes of baking time.

Serves 6.

8-oz. pkg. angel hair pasta, uncooked

12-1/2 oz. can chicken, drained and flaked

10-3/4 oz. can cream of chicken or celery soup

1 c. sour cream

1/2 c. onion, grated

1 t. garlic salt

1/8 t. Cajun seasoning or paprika

salt and pepper to taste

Optional: green peppers or green chiles, diced

1 to 2 c. shredded Cheddar cheese

1 to 2 2.8-oz. cans French fried onions

LINGUINE & ARTICHOKES IN WHITE SAUCE

**ANNETTE CERAVOLO
HOOVER, AL**

I have used this meatless recipe for many years, especially during Lent. Changed a few things to make easier without losing the flavor. I like to serve it with a zesty tossed salad.

- 16-oz. pkg. linguine pasta, uncooked
- 5 T. butter, sliced
- 6 T. extra-virgin olive oil
- 1 t. all-purpose flour
- 1 c. chicken broth
- 1 clove garlic, pressed
- 2 t. lemon juice
- 1 t. fresh parsley, minced
- salt and pepper to taste
- 14-oz. can quartered artichoke hearts, drained
- 3 T. grated Parmesan cheese
- 1 to 2 t. small capers, drained and rinsed
- Garnish: additional grated Parmesan cheese

Cook pasta according to package directions; drain. Meanwhile, in a large heavy skillet, melt butter with oil over low heat. Sprinkle with flour; cook and stir for 3 minutes. Increase heat to medium-high. Stir in broth; cook for one minute. Add garlic, lemon juice, parsley, salt and pepper; simmer over low heat for 5 minutes, stirring occasionally. Add artichokes, Parmesan cheese and capers; cover and simmer for 8 minutes. In a large serving dish, combine cooked pasta and artichoke mixture; toss together until well coated with sauce. Divide among 4 plates; top each with additional cheese.

Makes 4 servings.

MRS. PALMER'S FRIED CHICKEN

DEBBIE DONALDSON
ANDALUSIA, AL

This recipe brings back precious memories! Every time I fix this recipe I think of being a little girl watching my mama cook. She used the whole chicken, but I use boneless, skinless chicken breasts.

Cut chicken into strips, approximately 3 per breast. Place chicken in a large plastic zipping bag; pour buttermilk over chicken. Seal bag and chill for 2 to 3 hours. Drain chicken, discarding buttermilk; season chicken with salt and pepper. In a separate plastic zipping bag, combine flour and seasonings; seal bag and shake to mix well. Add chicken to bag, a few strips at a time; coat thoroughly. Heat oil to 350 degrees in an electric skillet. Carefully place chicken into hot oil; cook until both sides are golden. Drain on paper towels. Serve with chicken gravy or sweet-and-sour sauce.

Serves 4.

4 to 5 boneless, skinless chicken breasts
1 qt. buttermilk
salt and pepper to taste
2 c. self-rising flour
2 t. garlic powder
2 t. dried parsley
2 t. dried thyme
2 t. poultry seasoning
1 t. dried rosemary
1 t. pepper
1 qt. oil
Garnish: chicken gravy or sweet-and-sour sauce

DELICIOUS PULL-APART PIZZA BREAD

KAREN WALKER
BROOKWOOD, AL

Our family loves Alabama football and we love our finger foods too. This is a tasty new addition to serve along with other foods we have enjoyed over the years. We love it!

32-oz. pkg. pizza dough
1/3 c. garlic dipping oil
8-oz. pkg. sliced pepperoni
8-oz. pkg. shredded Mozzarella cheese
1 T. Italian seasoning
1/8 t. dried basil
Garnish: ranch salad dressing, garlic butter

Separate pizza dough into small bite-size pieces; place in a large bowl. Drizzle with dipping oil; toss dough pieces to lightly coat. Layer 1/3 of dough pieces in the bottom of a lightly greased Bundt® pan. Layer with half each of pepperoni and cheese; sprinkle with seasonings. Repeat layers, ending with dough pieces. Bake at 375 degrees for 30 to 40 minutes, until bread is golden and cooked through in the center. Remove from oven; invert pan onto a cutting board and turn out bread. To serve, pull bread apart into individual portions. Serve with dipping sauces as desired.

Serves 12.

ITALIAN SAUSAGE IN BEER

ANNETTE CERAVOLO
HOOVER, AL

I like to use both mild and hot sausage for this recipe, but if you're really brave, use only hot sausage. Either way, it's easy and delicious. It is also good as an appetizer.

In a deep skillet over medium-high heat, cook sausage for 5 to 7 minutes, until lightly golden. Drain, if needed. Add onion; cook for 5 to 6 minutes. Reduce heat to low. Stir in beer, hot sauce and parsley, if using. Simmer for 10 to 12 minutes, stirring every 3 to 4 minutes. Remove from heat. Transfer to a serving bowl. Freezes well for future use.

Makes 8 to 10 servings.

1 lb. mild Italian pork sausage link, cut into 1/2-inch pieces

1 lb. hot Italian pork sausage link, cut into 1/2-inch pieces

1 onion, minced

1 c. regular or non-alcoholic beer

1/2 t. hot pepper sauce

Optional: 1 T. fresh parsley, finely chopped

ROMANIAN SMOTHERED CHICKEN

MICHELLE POWELL
VALLEY, AL

My Mimi always made this for me on my trips home from college. It's one of the first dishes I learned to make for my family. I still serve it today, subbing Greek yogurt for some of the sour cream. Serve with a side of fresh green peas.

1/4 c. butter
3 lbs. boneless, skinless
   chicken breasts, cubed
2 T. all-purpose flour
1 T. onion, chopped
2 c. sour cream and/or
   plain Greek yogurt
salt and pepper to taste
1 c. sliced mushrooms
1 t. dried parsley
1 T. poppy seed
1 T. lemon juice cooked
   egg noodles
Garnish: paprika

Melt butter in a large skillet over medium-high heat. Cook chicken on all sides until golden; remove chicken to a bowl. Stir flour into remaining pan juices. Add onion and sour cream and/or yogurt; simmer over low heat for 3 to 5 minutes. Season with salt and pepper. Add mushrooms; return chicken to skillet. Stir in parsley and poppy seed. Cover and simmer over low heat about 30 minutes, until chicken is tender, stirring occasionally. Remove from heat; stir in lemon juice. Serve chicken and sauce over hot egg noodles, garnished with a sprinkle of paprika.

Makes 6 servings.

JUST FOR FUN

Mobile, Alabama used to be the capital of Louisiana. Mobile became part of Alabama on December 14, 1819.

DILLY HAM LOAVES

RHONDA LINK
LILLIAN, AL

We always had a huge turnout for the good food at our church's Day of Recollection luncheons. The ham loaves were especially liked. We served them with green beans, scalloped potatoes and creamed cucumbers. Our priest loved the ham loaves, but he wouldn't eat anything with onions in it, so we would grind them up real fine...he never knew they were there!

In a large bowl, combine ham and pork; mix well with your hands. Add milk, eggs, horseradish, one tablespoon mustard and dill; mix well. Add onion and all bread crumbs; mix again. Shape into 2 loaves; place each in an ungreased 9"x5" loaf pan. Combine water, vinegar, brown sugar and remaining mustard; pour over loaves. Spread jelly over loaves. Bake at 350 degrees for 1-1/2 hrs.

Makes 2 loaves; each serves 6 to 8.

2 lbs. cooked ham, ground

1 lb. ground pork

1 c. milk

2 eggs, beaten

1 T. horseradish sauce

1 T. plus 1 t. spicy brown mustard, divided

1-1/2 t. dill weed

1 onion, finely chopped

2 c. dry bread crumbs

1 c. panko bread crumbs

1/2 c. water

1/4 c. cider vinegar

1 c. brown sugar, packed

1/2 c. red raspberry or crabapple jelly, melted

SLOW-COOKER CHICKEN WITH PASTA

CONSTANCE LEWIS
FLORENCE, AL

Slow cooking keeps the chicken oh-so tender and moist.

4 boneless, skinless chicken breasts
1/4 t. salt
1/4 t. pepper
1 T. olive oil
14-1/2 oz. can crushed tomatoes
1/2 c. roasted red pepper, chopped
1 onion, chopped
1 clove garlic, minced
1/2 t. italian seasoning
1/2 c. milk
Garnish: Parmesean cheese

Sprinkle chicken with seasonings; set aside. Heat oil in a medium skillet over medium-high heat; add chicken and cook until golden on all sides. Arrange chicken in a slow cooker. In a small bowl, combine remaining ingredients except pasta and cheese; pour over chicken. Cover and cook on low setting for 7 to 9 hours, or on high setting for 3 to 4 hours. Cook pasta according to directions and serve chicken and juices overtop, and Parmesean cheese.

Makes 4 servings.

NO-FAIL FETTUCCINE ALFREDO

MICHELLE POWELL
VALLEY, AL

The easy no-cook sauce can be made ahead of time and refrigerated to top pasta or vegetables for a quick supper side.

16-oz. pkg. fettuccine pasta, uncooked
1/2 c. butter, softened
1/4 c. whipping cream
1/2 c. grated Parmesan cheese
salt and pepper to taste
Optional: additional Parmesan cheese

Cook pasta according to package directions; drain. Meanwhile, beat butter until fluffy; blend in cream a little at a time. Blend in cheese. Toss hot pasta with butter mixture; season with salt and pepper. Serve with additional cheese, if desired.

Serves 8.

BEEFY BEAN & CORN CASSEROLE

KATHERINE HARRISON
GOODWATER, AL

A favorite Monday dinner after a long weekend... my husband loves this!

In a skillet over medium heat, brown beef with onion and green pepper; drain. Stir in remaining ingredients except corn muffin mix. Transfer to a lightly greased 13"x9" baking pan; set aside. Prepare corn muffin mix according to package directions; spoon batter over beef mixture. Bake at 400 degrees for 20 to 30 minutes, until beef mixture is bubbly and topping is golden.

Makes 6 servings.

1-1/2 lbs. ground beef

1 onion, chopped

3/4 c. green pepper, chopped

15-1/2 oz. can chili beans in mild chili sauce

15-3/4 oz. can sweet corn & diced peppers, drained

14-1/2 oz. can diced tomatoes with green chiles, drained

1 c. barbecue sauce

1/2 t. salt

1/2 t. pepper

8-1/2 oz. pkg. corn muffin mix

FESTIVE TURKEY ENCHILADAS

CONSTANCE LEWIS
FLORENCE, AL

Zesty enchiladas filled with seasonal flavors.

2 to 2-1/2 c. cooked turkey, shredded

15-oz. can black beans, drained and rinsed

16-oz. can whole-berry cranberry sauce, divided

1-1/2 c. salsa, divided

1 c. shredded Colby-Jack cheese, divided

1/2 c. sour cream

3 green onions, sliced

1/4 c. fresh cilantro, snipped

1 t. ground cumin

1/2 t. salt

1/2 t. pepper

8 8-inch flour tortillas

1 t. hot pepper sauce

Optional: green onions, sliced

In a large bowl, stir together turkey, beans, one cup cranberry sauce, 1/2 cup salsa, 3/4 cup cheese, sour cream, green onions and seasonings. Spoon 2/3 cup filling onto each tortilla; roll up tortillas. Place seam-side down in a lightly greased 3-quart casserole dish; set aside. Stir together remaining cranberry sauce and salsa; add hot sauce and spoon over tortillas. Cover with aluminum foil; bake at 350 degrees for 45 minutes. Uncover; top with remaining cheese and bake an additional 5 to 10 minutes, until heated through and cheese is melted. Garnish with additional green onions, if desired.

Makes 8 servings.

GRANDMAMA'S CHICKEN & DRESSING

MARANDA ALLEN
ALEXANDER CITY, AL

This is the recipe my granny (great-grandmother) made... my grandmother just simplified it some. It's a tradition for our Thanksgiving and Christmas every year. Everybody is always saying how wonderful it is!

Cornbread may be made ahead of time. Crumble cornbread into bowl. In a saucepan, cover chicken with water; cook over medium-heat until tender. Cut chicken into cubes and add to bowl with cornbread. Add remaining ingredients; mix well. Mixture will be a little soupy. Transfer to a greased deep 13"x9" baking pan. Bake, uncovered, at 350 degrees for 30 minutes to one hour, until golden.

Makes 20 servings.

13"x9" pan homemade cornbread

4 chicken breasts

12-oz. pkg. herb-seasoned stuffing mix

2 14-oz. cans chicken broth

10-3/4 oz. can cream of chicken soup

4 eggs, beaten

1 T. butter, softened

1 c. milk

1 to 2 c. celery, chopped

1/2 to 1 c. onion, chopped

1/2 to 1 c. green pepper, chopped

SPICY SHRIMP PASTA

MICHELLE POWELL
VALLEY, AL

Growing up on the Gulf Coast, we've eaten shrimp cooked a bazillion ways. This is one of our favorites! It's quick & easy, too.

8-oz. linguine pasta, uncooked

2 T. olive oil

1 jalapeño pepper, seeds removed, finely chopped

2 cloves garlic, minced

1/2 t. salt

1/4 t. pepper

1 lb. medium shrimp, thawed if frozen, peeled and deveined

2 c. ripe tomatoes, chopped

Garnish: grated Parmesan cheese

Cook pasta according to package directions; drain. Meanwhile, in a large skillet, heat oil over medium high heat. Add jalapeño, garlic, salt and pepper. Cook and stir for one minute. Add shrimp; cook about 3 minutes, until shrimp turn opaque. Stir in tomatoes; heat through. Add cooked pasta; toss with shrimp mixture. Top with a sprinkle of Parmesan cheese.

Makes 4 servings.

KITCHEN TIP

To easily peel hard boiled eggs, add two eggs and just enough water to cover the eggs to a food storage container. Put the lid on and give it a few shakes. The shells will peel right off!

STUFFED CHICKEN BREASTS

URSALA ARMSTRONG
ODENVILLE, AL

Simple yet elegant...good enough for drop-in guests! Grill some asparagus spears along with the chicken for a simple side.

Flatten chicken breasts between wax paper. Spread each chicken breast with cream cheese and roll up. Wrap 2 slices bacon around each roll; secure with toothpicks. Place on a grill or in a grill pan over medium heat. Cook, turning occasionally, until golden and chicken juices run clear, about 20 to 25 minutes.

Serves 4.

4 boneless, skinless chicken
8 slices bacon breasts
8-oz. container garlic & herb cream cheese spread

COMPANY'S COMING CHICKEN

MICHELLE POWELL
VALLEY, AL

So delicious and impressive...but no one guesses how easy this is!

Place milk and bread crumbs in separate shallow bowls. Dip chicken into milk; coat in crumbs. Melt butter in a skillet over medium-high heat. Cook chicken on both sides until juices run clear. Remove to a plate; keep warm. Add chicken broth to skillet juices in skillet. Bring to a boil, stirring to loosen browned bits from the pan. Stir in cream and pimentos. Boil and stir for one minute. Reduce heat to medium-low. Add cheese, basil and pepper. Cook and stir until heated through. To serve, place chicken on egg noodles; spoon sauce from skillet over chicken.

Makes 4 servings.

1/4 c. milk
1/4 c. dry bread crumbs
4 boneless, skinless chicken breasts
3 T. butter
1/2 c. chicken broth
1 c. whipping cream
4-oz. jar sliced pimentos, drained
1/2 c. grated Parmesan cheese
2 T. dried basil
1/8 t. pepper
cooked egg noodles

SPAGHETTI PIE

**VICKIE
GOOSEBERRY PATCH**

*An old favorite! Sometimes I layer sliced mushrooms and black olives with
the other ingredients.*

**8-oz. pkg. spaghetti,
  uncooked & broken up
1 lb. ground beef
32-oz. jar pasta sauce
2 eggs, beaten
1/3 c. grated Parmesan
  cheese
3 c. cottage cheese,
  divided
1 c. shredded Italian-
  blend cheese, divided**

Cook spaghetti according to package directions,
just until tender; drain and return to pan. Meanwhile,
brown beef in a skillet over medium heat; drain.
Add sauce to beef; simmer over low heat for
several minutes. To spaghetti in pan, add eggs and
Parmesan cheese; stir gently to mix. Spoon 1/2 cup
sauce mixture into a slow cooker. Layer with half
each of spaghetti mixture, cottage cheese, remaining
sauce mixture and shredded cheese. Repeat
layering. Cover and cook on low setting for 6 to
8 hours.

Makes 6 servings.

FANCY FAUX CRAB

**MICHELLE MARBERRY
VALLEY, AL**

Quick, easy and impressive...perfect for company!

**2 cloves garlic, minced
2 T. butter
2 lbs. imitation
  crabmeat, flaked
1/2 c. chicken broth
8-oz. pkg. shredded
  Monterey Jack cheese
1 T. dried parsley
cooked angel hair pasta
  or rice**

In a skillet over medium-high heat, sauté garlic in
butter for one minute. Add crabmeat; cook for
4 minutes. With a slotted spoon, transfer crab to
a lightly greased 11"x7" baking pan; set aside and
keep warm. Add broth to skillet over medium heat;
bring to a boil. Cook and stir for 5 minutes, or until
broth is slightly reduced. Drizzle over crabmeat; top
with cheese and parsley. Bake, uncovered, at
350 degrees for 10 minutes, or until cheese is
melted. Serve over cooked pasta or rice.

Serves 6.

PINEAPPLE CHICKEN

DEBRA CROSBY
ELBA, AL

Serve with rice and Chinese stir-fry vegetables for a great meal.

Place chicken in slow cooker. Add salad dressing, pineapple and reserved juice. Cover and cook on high setting for 6 hours, or on low setting for 8 to 10 hours.

Serves 4 to 6.

3 to 4 lbs. boneless, skinless chicken

16-oz. bottle Catalina salad dressing

20-oz. can pineapple chunks, drained and 1/4 cup juice reserved

ITALIAN CRESCENT CASSEROLE

AMANDA GLADDEN
ONEONTA, AL

My family truly enjoys this crust-topped casserole...we like it better than spaghetti!

Brown meat and onion in a large skillet over medium heat. Drain; rinse meat mixture under hot water and return to skillet. Stir in sauce; simmer for about 10 minutes. Transfer mixture to a greased 13"x9" baking pan. Combine mozzarella cheese and sour cream; spoon over mixture in pan. Unroll crescent rolls but do not separate; place on top of mixture in pan. Drizzle rolls with melted butter; sprinkle with Parmesan cheese. Bake, uncovered, at 350 degrees for about 30 minutes, until bubbly and golden.

Serves 8.

1-1/2 to 2 lbs. ground beef or turkey

1 onion, chopped

16-oz. jar spaghetti sauce

8-oz. pkg. shredded mozzarella cheese

8-oz. container sour cream

8-oz. tube refrigerated crescent rolls

2 T. butter, melted

1/2 c. grated Parmesan cheese

SLOW-COOKED BEEF BRISKET

ANNETTE CERAVOLO
HOOVER, AL

A family-approved recipe...so good!

5-lb. whole beef brisket, trimmed

2 t. garlic, minced

1/2 t. pepper

2 onions, sliced 1/4-inch thick and separated into rings

12-oz. bottle chili sauce

2 T. Worcestershire sauce

1-1/2 c. dark ale or beef broth

1 T. brown sugar, packed

Optional: 3 to 4 redskin potatoes, quartered

Optional: 1 c. baby carrots

Place brisket fat-side down in a large slow cooker. Spread garlic evenly over brisket; sprinkle with pepper. Arrange onions over brisket; set aside. In a large bowl, combine sauces, ale or broth and brown sugar; pour mixture over brisket and onions. Cover and cook on low setting for 8 hours. Turn brisket over; stir onions into sauce and spoon sauce over brisket. Arrange potatoes and carrots around brisket, if desired. Cover and cook on low setting for an additional one to 2 hours, until brisket and vegetables are tender. Transfer brisket to a cutting board; tent with aluminum foil and let stand for 10 minutes. Stir liquid in slow cooker; spoon off fat and discard. If liquid is too thick, add water, a little at a time, to desired consistency. If too thin, pour into a saucepan; simmer, uncovered, over medium heat until thickened. Thinly slice brisket across the grain. Arrange on a serving platter, surrounded by vegetables, if using. Spoon cooking liquid over brisket before serving.

Makes 10 to 12 servings.

ITALIAN HAMBURGER MAC

BEN GOTHARD
JEMISON, AL

When I was a kid, my mom always made a dish like this...I could just eat the entire pot full. Now that I'm grown, I have put my own spin on the dish. This one's for you, Mama!

In a skillet over medium heat, cook beef until browned. Add onion, salt and pepper. Continue cooking for 5 minutes; drain. Transfer beef mixture to a stockpot; add uncooked macaroni and remaining ingredients. Bring to a boil over medium-high heat. Reduce heat; cover and simmer for about 20 minutes, stirring frequently, just until macaroni is tender. Remove from stove. Let cool for 10 minutes before serving to allow mixture to thicken.

Makes 8 to 10 servings.

- 2 lbs. ground beef chuck
- 1 onion, diced
- salt and pepper to taste
- 3 c. elbow macaroni, uncooked
- 2 46-oz. cans tomato juice
- 1 T. dried oregano
- 2 t. dried basil
- 1 t. garlic salt
- 1 t. onion salt

MUSTARD CHICKEN

JOY COLLINS
VESTAVIA, AL

This dish is easy and delicious! If I haven't made it for awhile, my husband will ask for it. It's easy to double or even triple if you're hosting a crowd or going to a potluck.

Mix together mayonnaise, butter and mustard in a shallow bowl. Place dry stuffing mix in a separate shallow bowl. Add chicken to mayonnaise mixture; coat well. Dip chicken into stuffing mix and press on both sides to coat. Arrange chicken in a lightly greased 13"x9" baking pan. Bake, covered, at 350 degrees for one hour. Uncover; bake for another 30 minutes, or until chicken juices run clear.

Makes 8 servings.

- 1/2 c. mayonnaise
- 1/2 c. butter, melted and slightly cooled
- 3 T. mustard
- 6-oz. pkg. herb-flavored stuffing mix
- 8 boneless, skinless chicken breasts

EVERYTHING-IN-THE-PANTRY CASSEROLE

CONSTANCE LEWIS
FLORENCE, AL

Mix a little of this, a little of that and enjoy!

1 lb. ground beef

2 t. poultry seasoning

2 t. dried thyme

1-1/2 t. ground cumin

salt and pepper to taste

2 t. garlic, minced

3 potatoes, thinly sliced

2 T. butter

1 onion, thinly sliced in rings

2 c. sliced mushrooms

10-3/4 oz. can cream of chicken soup

3/4 c. water

20 saltine crackers, crushed

Garnish: 1/8 t. paprika

Place ground beef in a large skillet; sprinkle with seasonings and garlic. Heat, stirring frequently, over medium heat until browned. Drain; transfer to an ungreased 13"x9" baking dish. Arrange 2 layers of sliced potatoes over beef mixture, sprinkling each layer with salt and pepper; set aside. Melt butter in the skillet over medium heat; sauté onion and mushrooms until crisp-tender. Spread over potatoes; set aside. Combine soup and water; spread evenly over casserole. Top with cracker crumbs and sprinkle with paprika. Cover with aluminum foil and bake for one hour, or until potatoes are soft. Remove foil and bake an additional 10 minutes, or until golden.

Serves 4 to 6.

ITALIAN SPINACH LASAGNA

MARY HUGHES
TALLADEGA, AL

Perfect for a busy day with company coming for dinner. Not having to precook the lasagna noodles is a bonus.

In a large bowl, combine ricotta cheese, one cup mozzarella cheese, 1/4 cup Parmesan cheese, spinach, eggs and soup mix. Stir well and set aside. Spread one cup pasta sauce in a large slow cooker. Layer with 4 lasagna noodles, broken to fit; add one cup pasta sauce and half of ricotta mixture. Repeat; top with remaining lasagna noodles and 2 cups pasta sauce. Reserve remaining cheeses and pasta sauce in the refrigerator. Cover and cook on low setting for 5 to 6 hours. Sprinkle with remaining cheeses; cover and cook on low setting an additional 10 minutes. Let stand 10 minutes before serving; cut into wedges. Heat remaining pasta sauce; ladle over portions of lasagna.

Makes 8 servings.

- 2 15-oz. containers ricotta cheese
- 8-oz. pkg. shredded Mozzarella cheese, divided
- 1/2 c. grated Parmesan cheese, divided
- 10-oz. pkg. frozen chopped spinach, thawed and squeezed dry
- 2 eggs, beaten
- 1-oz. pkg. vegetable soup mix
- 2 24-oz. jars favorite pasta sauce, divided
- 12 lasagna noodles, uncooked and divided

CHAPTER FIVE

OLYMPIC WINNER

Appetizers & Snacks

WHETHER YOU ARE HAVING COMPANY OR JUST NEED A LITTLE SNACK TO HOLD YOU OVER UNTIL THE NEXT MEAL, YOU'LL FIND THESE RECIPES ARE GREAT FOR TAKING ON-THE-GO OR AS A FAVORITE APPETIZER.

ITALIAN FRIED GREEN TOMATOES

DEBRA ELLIOTT
TRUSSVILLE, AL

When I was growing up in the south, my grandma would always cook sweet fried green tomatoes for Sunday supper, and their yummy goodness melted in my mouth. This recipe is a sassy twist on my grandma's recipe and is one of my family's favorite Sunday supper side dishes.

3 firm green tomatoes, each cut into 4 slices

1 to 2 c. all-purpose flour

1 T. garlic powder

1 t. dried oregano

2 eggs, beaten

2 c. buttermilk

2 c. Italian-seasoned dry bread crumbs

salt and pepper to taste

shortening or lard for frying

Garnish: chipotle mayonnaise, crumbled feta cheese

Place tomato slices in a bowl of ice water; set aside. In a shallow bowl, combine flour and seasonings; mix well. In a separate shallow bowl, whisk together eggs and buttermilk. Spread bread crumbs on a plate. Drain tomatoes; pat dry with paper towels. Season both sides of tomato slices with salt and pepper. Coat tomato slices with flour mixture; dip in egg mixture. Coat with bread crumbs, pushing down to coat thoroughly. Melt shortening or lard in a large cast-iron skillet over medium heat. Add tomatoes to skillet, 4 slices at a time. Cook on each side until fork-tender and golden. Remove to paper towels to drain. Drizzle slices with chipotle mayonnaise; sprinkle with feta cheese. Serve warm.

Makes 4 to 8 servings.

MOM'S SUPER-QUICK CHEESE BALL

ROBYN STROH
CALERA, AL

My mother always made this for our Christmas Eve and New Year's Eve get-togethers. You can customize it with your favorite flavor of salsa, and it's so easy!

In a bowl, combine cream cheese and salsa until smooth. Add shredded cheese. Line a separate bowl with plastic wrap; transfer cream cheese mixture to bowl. Cover and refrigerate until firm. (May put into freezer to speed up the process.) Lift cheese ball in plastic wrap onto the counter; open up plastic wrap and sprinkle cheese ball with chopped pecans. Roll cheese ball until covered with nuts. Re-wrap with plastic wrap and return to refrigerator.

Makes 10 to 12 servings.

8-oz. pkg. cream cheese, softened

1/2 c. medium or hot salsa

8-oz. pkg. finely shredded sharp Cheddar cheese

1/2 c. chopped pecans

DINNERTIME CONVERSATION

Alabama is known for its strong hand in the civil rights movement. In 1955 two black American activist women were arrested when they refused to give up their bus seats for a white person which was the law at that time.

BAKED MUSHROOM DIP

VICKIE
GOOSEBERRY PATCH

A delicious warm dip that our guests love, and an easy make-ahead.
Assemble it but don't bake, cover and refrigerate up to two days.
Uncover and bake for serving.

2 T. butter

3 c. mushrooms, chopped

1 c. onion, finely chopped

1 clove garlic, minced

8-oz. pkg. cream cheese, softened and cubed

1/2 t. dried dill weed

1/2 t. seasoned salt

pepper to taste

1-1/2 c. shredded Pepper Jack cheese

1/2 c. mayonnaise

Optional: snipped fresh chives

baguette slices or pita chips

Melt butter in a large skillet over medium heat; add mushrooms, onion and garlic. Cook for 10 minutes, or until mushrooms are golden and liquid is evaporated. Reduce heat to low. Add cream cheese and seasonings; cook and stir until cream cheese is melted. Add shredded cheese and mayonnaise; mix well. Spread mixture in an ungreased 9" pie plate or shallow casserole dish. Bake, uncovered, at 350 degrees for about 30 minutes, until hot and bubbly. Garnish with chives, if desired; serve with baguette slices or pita chips.

Makes about 2-1/2 cups.

CHEESY SAUSAGE DIP

DEBRA COLLINS
GAYLESVILLE, AL

This is an awesome dip for any party!

In a skillet over medium heat, brown sausage; drain and set aside. In a slow cooker, combine cream cheese, sour cream, tomatoes with juice and Cheddar cheese. Cover and cook on low setting for one hour, or until cheeses are melted. Stir in spinach, sausage and garlic powder. Cover and cook on low setting for one to 2 hours longer, until dip is smooth and warmed through.

Serves 10 to 15.

1 lb. ground pork sausage

8-oz. pkg. cream cheese, cubed

8-oz. container sour cream

10-oz. can diced tomatoes with green chiles

1 c. shredded Cheddar cheese

10-oz. pkg. frozen spinach, thawed and drained

1/2 t. garlic powder

PRESENTATION

Serve up caramel or chocolate ice cream sauces along side of salty snacks for a fun and flavorful dipping option.

HAWAIIAN BOWL DIP

SHERRY HILL
SYLACAUGA, AL

My grandmother and I made this hot dip when I was in my teen years and I have been making it ever since. My family really enjoys it in the cool fall months, just in time for football. It is delicious and easy to make...everyone enjoys it.

16-oz. loaf Hawaiian
  sweet bread
8-oz. pkg. cream cheese,
  softened
12-oz. container sour
  cream
2 c. shredded sharp
  Cheddar cheese
2 c. shredded mild
  Cheddar cheese
1 bunch green onions,
  chopped
2-oz. pkg. deli honey
  ham, chopped
scoop-type corn chips

Leave bread in its aluminum foil pan. Cut off the top of bread and reserve. Scoop out the inside to make a bowl; set aside. In a bowl, blend cream cheese and sour cream. Fold in remaining ingredients except corn chips. Spoon mixture into hollowed-out bread; replace bread top. Wrap bread completely in foil. Bake at 350 degrees for one hour. Just before serving, remove bread top and stir dip very well. Serve with corn chips.

Serves 8 to 10.

JUST FOR FUN

The Mobile–Tensaw River Delta is the largest river delta and wetland in Alabama. It stretches more than 391 square miles, and is the second largest delta in the United States!

SWEET FRIED GREEN TOMATOES

**KANDACE GILES
SYLACAUGA, AL**

This recipe is half mine and half my grandmother's. One night we were having dinner at her house and she was making fried green tomatoes. Instead of grabbing the flour, she grabbed pancake mix! These turned out to be a sweeter version of the usual fried green tomatoes...so delicious!

In a large bowl, mix together cornmeal, pancake mix, salt and pepper; set aside. Beat eggs in a separate large bowl. Dip each tomato slice into eggs, add to cornmeal mixture and coat tomatoes on both sides. To a large skillet over medium heat, add 1/2-inch oil. Add 4 to 5 coated tomatoes to oil at a time; cook until golden on both sides. Remove tomatoes to a paper towel-lined plate. Let cool about 2 minutes before serving.

1 c. cornmeal
1 c. pancake mix
1 T. salt
1 T. pepper
2 eggs
4 green tomatoes, sliced to desired thickness
oil for frying

Serves 4.

EASY RANCH CHEESE BALL

**CAROLYN TYLER
HAMILTON, AL**

I came up with this recipe one day when I needed an appetizer to take to a get-together. It was a hit! It's really simple to make... great for new cooks.

2 8-oz. pkgs. cream cheese, softened

1-oz. pkg. ranch salad dressing mix

Optional: 1 bunch green onions, chopped

3/4 c. bacon bits or chopped pecans

assorted crackers or cut-up vegetables

In a large bowl, combine cream cheese, dip mix and onions, if using. Blend thoroughly and form into a ball. Wrap in plastic wrap; refrigerate at least 2 hours, until firm. Just before serving time, roll cheese ball in bacon bits or pecans on a length of wax paper. Serve cheese ball with crackers or vegetables.

Makes 15 to 25 servings.

CAJUN BOILED PEANUTS

MICHELLE MARBERRY
VALLEY, AL

A tailgating staple in the South! Leave out the crab boil and hot sauce if you prefer them plain. These may take a little time to make in the slow cooker, but they're definitely worth it!

Combine all ingredients in a 6-quart slow cooker. Cover and cook on high setting for 18 hours, or until peanuts are soft. Drain and serve.

Makes about 2 pounds.

2 lbs. raw peanuts in shells
1/2 c. hot pepper sauce
1 c. salt
12 c. water
3-oz. pkg. crab boil seasoning mix

SPICY BROCCOMOLE

MICHELLE POWELL
VALLEY, AL

A delicious, creamy dip or topping for tacos, burritos and quesadillas that's high-protein, low-cal and low-fat. For an extra-spicy flavor, leave in some of the jalapeño seeds.

In a saucepan over medium-high heat, cook broccoli in salted water until very soft. Drain well, squeezing out water with a paper towel. Transfer broccoli to a food processor or blender; add remaining ingredients. Process until smooth. If a smoother texture is desired, add a little more olive oil. Serve warm.

Makes 10 servings, or about 3 cups.

3 c. fresh or frozen broccoli flowerets
1 jalapeño pepper, roasted, seeded and chopped
1 green onion, chopped
1/3 c. plain Greek yogurt
3 T. fresh cilantro, chopped
1 t. olive oil
1/4 t. chili powder
1/4 t. garlic powder
1/4 t. salt
1/4 t. pepper

DEEP-FRIED PIMENTO CHEESE & CELERY BITES

**DEBRA ELLIOT
TRUSSVILLE, AL**

Growing up in the south, I ate a lot of pimento cheese on celery. I took a southern classic and turned it into deep-fried goodness.

12-oz. container pimento cheese

1 stalk celery, finely chopped

1 egg, beaten

1/2 c. Italian-seasoned dry bread crumbs

1 t. seasoned salt

1/2 t. paprika

1/4 c. all-purpose flour

2 to 3 c. oil for deep frying

Garnish: ranch salad dressing

In a bowl, combine cheese, celery, egg, bread crumbs and seasoning; mix well and set aside. Place flour in a shallow dish. Lightly spray an ice cream scoop with non-stick vegetable spray. Scoop cheese mixture into small balls; roll balls in flour to coat lightly. Add oil to a deep fryer, filling about 3/4 full; heat to 375 degrees. Working in batches, add cheese balls and cook until golden. Remove to paper towels to drain. Serve with salad dressing.

Serves 12 to 16.

PRESENTATION

To keep outdoor table coverings in place, tie tablecloths to the table legs with pretty ribbon.

KAY'S BEST CHEESE BALL

KAY TURNER
SLOCOMB, AL

I have made this cheese ball every Thanksgiving, Christmas and Easter meal for my family for many years. It's a huge hit...friends will invite me to dinner and ask me to bring my cheese ball! Sometimes I add finely chopped pecans instead of the beef.

In a large bowl, combine cream cheese, half of beef and remaining ingredients except crackers. Mix very well, using your hands. Form into a ball and place on a serving plate. Cover with remaining beef. Cover with plastic wrap; refrigerate overnight. Serve with crackers.

Makes one large cheese ball.

- 2 8-oz. pkgs. cream cheese, room temperature
- 2 2-oz. pkgs. sliced beef, chopped and divided
- 3 T. mayonnaise
- 4 to 5 green onions, finely chopped
- 1 t. Dijon or yellow mustard
- 1 T. garlic salt
- snack crackers

PARTY CORN DIP

WHITNEY BURGESS
FLORENCE, AL

This is my go-to recipe for any party. It's so simple, fast and always a crowd-pleaser!

Partially drain each can of corn and tomatoes, leaving about half the liquid in each can. Pour corn and tomatoes with remaining liquid into a slow cooker; add cream cheese. Cover and cook on low setting for one to 2 hours, stirring occasionally, until cream cheese is melted and dip is warmed through. Serve warm with corn chips for dipping.

Serves 8 to 10.

- 3 15-oz. cans shoepeg corn
- 3 10-oz. cans diced tomatoes with green chiles
- 3 8-oz. pkgs. cream cheese, cubed
- corn chips

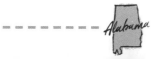

AMAZING CHEESE DIP

KIM CURRIER
HUNTSVILLE, AL

*I got this recipe from a dear friend of mine, Sindy. Each time I make it,
I think of Sindy and the love she has for her family & friends. Be sure
to have heaps of tortilla chips ready...this recipe serves a crowd!*

1 lb. ground pork
  sausage or ground
  beef
16-oz. pkg. pasteurized
  process cheese spread,
  cubed
10-3/4 oz. can cream of
  chicken soup
10-3/4 oz. can cream of
  celery soup
10-oz. can diced
  tomatoes with green
  chiles
tortilla chips

In a skillet, brown sausage or beef over medium heat until no longer pink; drain. In a saucepan, melt cheese over medium-low heat. Once cheese is completely melted, stir in soups, tomatoes with juice and sausage or beef. Stir to blend. Serve warm with tortilla chips.

Serves 10 to 12.

HOMEMADE PIMENTO CHEESE

CORA PHILLIPS
OZARK, AL

If you have never eaten homemade pimento cheese, you are being deprived. It is nothing like the store-bought kind. The little touch of onion and the sweetness from the glazed pecans sets this recipe above the rest...and it's easy-peasy!

In a bowl, mix all ingredients together, blending well. Cover and refrigerate overnight. Serve with snack crackers.

Serves 18 to 20.

- 3 c. finely shredded Cheddar cheese
- 4-oz. jar diced pimentos, drained
- 1-1/2 c. mayonnaise
- 2 T. onion, finely minced
- 1 T. Worcestershire sauce
- 1 t. hot pepper sauce
- 1/4 t. cayenne pepper
- 1/2 c. glazed pecans, chopped

DINNERTIME CONVERSATION

Birmingham, Alabama is the birthplace of a famous track-and-field athlete, who won nine Olympic gold medals during the 1980s and '90s, won one Olympic silver medal, and ten World Championship medals, including eight gold.

CHEDDAR-PECAN SPREAD

ANNETTE CERAVOLO
HOOVER, AL

*This spread is such a hit at family get-togethers or entertaining
friends that I always double the recipe! It can be made the day
before...a handy make-ahead.*

3/4 c. mayonnaise

1/2 c. pecans, toasted
and finely chopped

4 slices bacon, crisply
cooked and finely
chopped

2 T. green onions, finely
chopped

8-oz. pkg. shredded
Cheddar cheese

bread slices or crackers

In a bowl, stir together mayonnaise, pecans, bacon
and onions until well combined. Add cheese; blend
well. Pack into a small serving bowl. Cover and chill
for 2 hours to overnight. Serve at room temperature
with bread or crackers.

Makes 2 cups.

LITTLE SUGAR PIGGIES

CANDACE HEAD
HALEYVILLE, AL

*Warning! You can't eat just one of these scrumptious little treats...plus,
it's such an easy slow-cooker recipe.*

30 hot dogs

2 lbs. bacon wooden
toothpicks

16-oz. pkg. light brown
sugar

Optional: 3 to 4 shakes
hot pepper sauce

Cut hot dogs and bacon slices into 3 to 4 equal
pieces each. Wrap each hot dog piece with a piece
of bacon; secure with a toothpick. Transfer wrapped
hot dogs to a slow cooker. Add brown sugar and hot
sauce, if using, to slow cooker. Cover and cook on
low setting, stirring occasionally, for 5 to 6 hours,
until bacon is cooked.

Serves 25 to 30.

Alabama — — — — — — —

STUFFED JALAPEÑO PEPPERS

DONNA RIGGINS
BOAZ, AL

These are amazing! Great for any occasion. I fix these during football season.

Brown sausage in a skillet over medium heat; drain. Add cream cheese and mix well. Spoon mixture into pepper halves. Arrange on a greased baking sheet. Bake at 350 degrees for 10 to 12 minutes, until bubbly and tender. Top with Cheddar cheese; bake another 3 to 5 minutes, until cheese has melted.

Serves 16 to 20.

1 lb. ground pork sausage

1/2 to 3/4 c. shredded Cheddar cheese

8-oz. pkg. cream cheese, softened

8 to 10 jalapeño peppers, halved and seeded

TUSCAN VALLEY DIP

ANNETTE CERAVOLO
HOOVER, AL

Perfected over the years, this dip is so creamy and filled with savory flavor. It's always popular at parties...guests will definitely be asking you for the recipe.

In a bowl, stir together cream cheese and sour cream until well blended. Add tomatoes, olives and onion; mix well. Cover and refrigerate 8 hours to overnight so flavors can blend. Let stand at room temperature for 30 minutes before serving. Serve with crackers and vegetables.

Makes 4 cups.

2 8-oz. pkgs. cream cheese, softened

2 T. sour cream

3/4 c. sun-dried tomatoes (not oil-packed), finely chopped

1 c. sliced black olives, drained

1/4 c. red onion, finely chopped

assorted crackers and cut-up vegetables

CHAPTER SIX

HEART OF DIXIE
Desserts

THERE IS ALWAYS ROOM FOR
DESSERT. SO WHEN YOUR SWEET
TOOTH IS CALLING, THESE SIMPLE
SWEETS ARE THE PERFECT WAY
TO END THE DAY.

BERRY-RHUBARB PIE

**NICHOLE LEIGHTON
MONTGOMERY, AL**

*My husband loves rhubarb, so when the season comes it's an endless
parade of rhubarb dishes. I just made up this new version. Now we have
a pie we love more than any other!*

2 9-inch pie crusts,
  unbaked
1 T. all-purpose flour
2 T. instant tapioca,
  uncooked
1-1/4 c. sugar
1/2 t. cinnamon
2-1/2 c. rhubarb, chopped
1-1/2 c. fresh
  strawberries, hulled
  and chopped
1-1/2 c. fresh
  blackberries
1/2 t. lime zest
1 t. lime juice
1 t. vanilla extract
2 T. butter, diced
1 egg white
1 t. water

Arrange one pie crust in a 9-inch pie plate; set
aside. Combine flour, tapioca, sugar and cinnamon.
In a separate bowl, combine rhubarb, berries, zest,
juice and vanilla. Add flour mixture; stir gently to coat
fruit. Spoon fruit into crust; dot with butter. Cover with
remaining crust; pinch to seal and cut vents. Whisk
together egg white and water; brush over crust. Bake
at 375 degrees for 50 to 60 minutes, until crust is
golden.

Serves 8.

PINEAPPLE PUDDING

DEBRA ELLIOTT
BIRMINGHAM, AL

This pineapple pudding is my favorite. It's an easy-to-make, mouthwatering dessert that will tickle your taste buds.

Layer wafers in a large glass trifle bowl until bottom is covered, reserving 8 to 10 for garnish. In a saucepan over medium heat, combine sugar, cornstarch and salt. Stir in milk. Cook, stirring occasionally, until mixture thickens. Add vanilla and cook for 2 to 3 minutes. Once mixture is thick, fold in crushed pineapple. Spread pudding mixture over wafers in bowl; let cool. Top pudding with whipped topping. Garnish with pineapple slices, reserved wafers and cherries.

Serves 6.

- 12-oz. pkg. vanilla wafers, divided
- 1/3 c. sugar
- 3 T. cornstarch
- 1/4 t. salt
- 2-1/2 c. milk
- 1-1/2 t. vanilla extract
- 20-oz. can crushed pineapple, drained
- 8-oz. container frozen whipped topping, thawed
- Garnish: pineapple slices, maraschino cherries

DINNERTIME CONVERSATION

On April 15, 1886, Montgomery, Alabama became the first U.S. city to initiate a city-wide electric streetcar system for transportation. It was known as the Capital City Street Railway or the "Lightning Route." The system was retired after only 50 years of service and was replaced by buses.

BEST-EVER LEMON BARS

MICHELE MARBERRY
VALLEY, AL

*I make these for my Mimi. She's very particular about lemon desserts,
so when she says these are the best, I believe her!*

1/2 c. butter, melted
1-1/4 c. plus 2 T. sugar,
  divided
3/4 t. vanilla extract
1/8 t. salt
1 c. plus
3 T. all-purpose flour
3 eggs, beaten
1-1/2 t. lemon zest
1/2 c. lemon juice
Garnish: powdered
  sugar

Stir together butter, 1/4 cup sugar, vanilla and salt.
Add one cup flour; mix just until incorporated. Press
evenly into the bottom of an aluminum foil-lined
8"x8" baking pan. Place a rack in the lower 1/3 of
oven. Bake at 350 degrees for 25 to 30 minutes,
until edges are golden and center is lightly golden.
While crust is baking, stir together remaining sugar
and flour in a separate bowl. Whisk in eggs; stir in
lemon zest and juice. When baked crust is done,
reduce oven temperature to 300 degrees. Pull out
oven rack without removing pan; pour lling over hot
crust. Bake for 20 to 25 minutes longer, until topping
is puffed at the edges and no longer jiggles in the
center. Set pan on a wire rack; cool completely.
Lift the ends of the foil; transfer to a cutting board.
Cut into bars with a long sharp knife. Keep bars
refrigerated in an airtight container up to 3 days.
Dust with powdered sugar at serving time.

Makes 16 bars.

CHOCOLATE PUDDING CAKE

ANNETTE CERAVOLO
HOOVER, AL

A double dose of chocolate that's been a family favorite for years!

Prepare cake according to package directions. Pour batter into a greased 13"x9" baking pan; set aside. In a separate bowl, combine water, milk, pudding mixes and sugar. Whisk together for 2 minutes, or well blended; pour over batter. Set pan in a larger shallow pan to catch drips. Bake at 350 degrees for 55 minutes to one hour, until a toothpick tests clean. Cool for 20 minutes. "Sauce" on top will thicken slightly as it cools. Serve warm, spooned into bowls and garnished as desired.

Makes 12 servings.

- 18-1/2 oz. pkg. devil's food cake mix
- 1-1/4 c. water
- 2 c. milk
- 2 3.9-oz. pkgs. instant chocolate pudding mix
- 1/3 c. sugar
- Optional: whipped topping or vanilla ice cream

JUST FOR FUN

The name Alabama came from the Alabama River. The origin of the word Alabama is from two words "Alba and Amo". Alba refers to vegetables, herbs, and plants while Amo refers to gatherer. The combination of these words "vegetation gatherer" describes the Alabama Indians who were the early settlers in the region.

CARAMEL APPLE CIDER

MICHELLE MARBERRY
VALLEY, AL

Tailgaters and trick-or-treaters love this drink on a crisp fall night!

64-oz. bottle apple cider
1/2 c. caramel ice cream topping
1/2 t. cinnamon
Garnish: whipped cream, cinnamon, additional caramel topping, cinnamon sticks

Combine all ingredients except garnish in a slow cooker. Cover and cook on low setting for 3 to 4 hours. Ladle hot cider into mugs; top with a dollop of whipped cream, a sprinkle of cinnamon and a drizzle of caramel topping. Serve with a cinnamon stick for stirring.

8 servings.

CHOCOLATE COBBLER

CHRISTY BONNER
BERRY, AL

This is a treasured family recipe that has been passed down for many years...a rich, scrumptious treat for chocolate lovers!

3/4 c. margarine, melted
1-1/2 c. self-rising flour
2-1/2 c. sugar, divided
1/2 c. plus 1 T. baking cocoa, divided
3/4 c. milk
1 t. vanilla extract
2-1/4 c. boiling water

Spread margarine in a 13"x9" glass baking pan; set aside. Combine flour, one cup sugar, 3 tablespoons cocoa, milk and vanilla; pour into pan. Mix together remaining sugar and cocoa; sprinkle over top. Pour boiling water over top; do not stir. Bake at 350 degrees for 40 to 45 minutes.

Makes 12 to 14 servings.

YA YA'S YUM YUM

AMANDA SPEARS
DECATUR, AL

This was my great-great-grandmother's recipe. She loved to bake and her pie safe was always filled with scrumptious baked goodies and treats. She passed her love for baking on to me. I only hope I am half as good a baker as she was! She used her own homemade biscuits for this recipe, but I have found refrigerated biscuits work well and save time too.

Spray an 11"x9" baking pan with non-stick vegetable spray. Line pan with quartered biscuits; set aside. In a bowl, combine brown sugar and 1/2 cup melted butter; spoon over biscuits. Spoon pie filling over the top. Bake at 325 degrees for 25 to 30 minutes; do not open oven while baking. Remove from oven; set aside. In another bowl, mix together cream cheese and remaining melted butter; stir in powdered sugar and condensed milk. Spread over cherries and serve.

Makes 6 servings.

2 16.3-oz. tubes refrigerated flaky buttermilk biscuits, quartered

1/2 c. brown sugar, packed

3/4 c. butter, melted and divided

2 21-oz. cans cherry pie filling

1/2 c. cream cheese, softened

1-1/2 c. powdered sugar

14-oz. can sweetened condensed milk

CHOCOLATEY COCOA GRAVY

LINDA RHOADES
GARDENDALE, AL

Ladle this over hot buttered biscuits.it is great! I first ate this at my grandmother's house, and it became a family favorite. Use heaping tablespoonfuls of flour and cocoa.

1 c. sugar
1 T. all-purpose flour
2 c. water
1 T. baking cocoa

Mix all ingredients together in a saucepan. Cook and stir over medium heat until thickened.

Makes 3 cups.

BUTTER & NUT POUND CAKE

ROBYN STROH
CALERA, AL

When I was a little girl, my mom used to make this cake often. Once I became a teenager, I made it so often that I had the recipe memorized. Now that I am a wife and mother, this is my husband's favorite pound cake. It is so delicious!

1 c. butter, softened
2 c. sugar
4 eggs
1/2 c. self-rising flour
2-1/2 c. all-purpose flour
1 c. milk
1 to 2 T. vanilla, butter
   & nut flavoring

In a large bowl, blend together butter and sugar until light and fluffy. Add eggs, one at a time, beating after each addition. Add self-rising flour; mix well. Add all-purpose flour alternately with milk, ending with flour. Beat until well combined after each addition. Stir in flavoring. Transfer batter to a greased and floured Bundt® pan. Bake at 325 degrees for one hour and 10 to 15 minutes.

Makes 12 to 16 servings.

GRANNY'S CHOCOLATE FUDGE

CHRISTY BONNER
BERRY, AL

This is a family recipe that my granny passed down to me. She received this recipe from a dear friend of hers in El Paso, Texas, when my Papaw was serving in the war. It has never failed me and always turns out scrumptious.

In a large, heavy saucepan over medium-high heat, combine sugar, margarine and evaporated milk. Bring to a rolling boil; boil for 5 minutes, stirring constantly. Remove from heat; add remaining ingredients. Stir until smooth and chocolate is melted. Pour onto a greased 15"x10" jelly-roll pan. Let stand overnight, or until firm. Cut into one-inch squares.

Makes 5 pounds.

- 4-1/2 c. sugar
- 1-1/2 c. margarine
- 12-oz. can evaporated milk
- 3 6-oz. pkgs. semi-sweet chocolate chips
- 1 t. vanilla extract
- 13-oz. jar marshmallow creme
- 2 c. chopped pecans or walnuts

RAISIN ROCKS

CAROLYN BRITTON
MILLRY, AL

*My grandmother always made these spicy fruit & nut cookies for the
holidays...they went perfectly with her ambrosia salad.*

1-1/2 c. brown sugar,
  packed
2/3 c. butter-flavored
  shortening
2 eggs
1 t. vanilla extract
2-1/2 c. all-purpose flour
1 t. baking soda
1/4 t. salt
1 t. cinnamon
1/4 t. ground cloves
3 c. chopped pecans
1-1/2 c. raisins

In a large bowl, blend together brown sugar and
shortening until light and fluffy. Add eggs one at a
time; beat well after each. Stir in vanilla; set aside.
In a separate bowl, sift together dry ingredients.
Gradually add flour mixture to brown sugar mixture;
mix well. Fold in pecans and raisins. Drop by
teaspoonfuls onto parchment paper-lined baking
sheets. Bake at 325 degrees for 10 to 15 minutes,
until golden.

Makes 6 dozen.

CARAMEL FONDUE

MICHELLE MARBERRY
VALLEY, AL

*Yum...this sweet dip is perfect party fare! It makes a delectable ice cream
topping too.*

2 14-oz. pkgs. caramels,
  unwrapped
2 14-oz. cans sweetened
  condensed milk
apple and pear slices,
  banana chunks,
  marshmallows, pound
  cake cubes

Combine caramels and condensed milk in a slow
cooker that has been sprayed with non-stick
vegetable spray. Cover and cook on low setting for
3-1/2 hours, stirring occasionally, or until caramels
are melted and mixture is smooth. Serve with a
choice of dippers.

Makes 4-1/2 cups.

SUNDAE CAKE

SHARLENE CASTEEL
FORT MITCHELL, AL

We take this luscious cake to church meetings, and it is enjoyed by all...it is addictive! Make it a day early so it can chill well.

Bake cake mix according to package directions, using a greased 13"x9" baking pan. When cake is cool, poke holes in the top with the handle of a wooden spoon. Drizzle chocolate syrup over cake. Top with whipped topping and pecans. Drizzle caramel syrup over cake. For best flavor, cover and refrigerate 8 hours to overnight. Cut into squares to serve.

Makes 18 to 24 servings.

16-1/2 oz. pkg. golden butter cake mix

1 c. chocolate syrup

8-oz. container frozen whipped topping, thawed

1/2 c. chopped pecans

caramel ice cream topping to taste

HOT LEMONADE

MICHELLE MARBERRY
VALLEY, AL

Not medicine, but it sure feels good on a scratchy winter throat.

Combine all ingredients except garnish in a slow cooker. Cover and cook on low setting for 3 hours. Whisk well. Ladle into mugs; serve with cinnamon sticks for stirring.

Makes 9 servings.

4 c. water

juice of 14 lemons, or 3 c. lemon juice

2 c. sugar

1/4 c. honey

Garnish: cinnamon sticks

GRAN JAN'S ICE CREAM BROWNIES

JANICE FRY
HOOVER, AL

I love to make this for holidays and when the grandkids come over. I had written under the recipe: "This was the hit of Bible School workers in 1996! Everyone loved it!" And, of course, for the next few years I was asked to take it for the helpers at church. It's a great dessert to make ahead during the holidays when you are busy. It's delicious, easy and everybody loves it!

2 3.6-oz. pkg. fudge brownie mix

1/2 gal. vanilla ice cream, softened

FROSTING:

1-1/2 c. evaporated milk

1/2 c. butter, sliced

2/3 c. semi-sweet chocolate chips

2 c. powdered sugar

1 t. vanilla extract

1-1/2 c. chopped pecans or walnuts

Prepare brownie mix according to package directions, adding ingredients called for. Bake in a lightly greased 13"x9" baking pan; let cool in pan. Spread ice cream over brownies; cover and freeze until hardened. Spread Chocolate Frosting over ice cream; cover again and return to freezer. Remove from freezer 5 to 10 minutes before serving. Cut into squares.

Chocolate Frosting:

In a large saucepan over medium-high heat, combine evaporated milk, butter, chocolate chips and powdered sugar. Bring to a boil, stirring until smooth. Reduce heat to medium and cook for 8 minutes. Remove from heat; stir in vanilla and nuts. Let cool before using.

Makes 12 to 15 servings.

CHRISTMAS CANDY RED STRAWBERRIES

FAY MELTON
SHEFIELD, AL

*These berries look so sweet packed in green lattice strawberry baskets!
I save empty berry baskets over the summer to present as gifts.*

Beat together gelatin mixes and condensed milk in a large bowl until smooth. Add pecans, coconut and vanilla; stir just until combined. Shape into strawberries; roll sides of strawberries in red sugar and dip tops into green sugar. Tint almonds with green food coloring and insert one into the top of each berry for the stem. Store in an airtight container in refrigerator.

Makes 2 dozen.

2 3-oz. pkg's. strawberry gelatin mix
1/2 c. sweetened condensed milk
1 c. pecans, finely chopped
1 c. sweetened flaked coconut
1 t. vanilla extract
red and green decorating sugar
1/3 c. slivered almonds
few drops green food coloring

PRESENTATION

For a fruity twist, instead of fruit salad in a bowl, layer diced fruit onto skewers and place them on a pretty tray or plate.

DIXIE-LANE CAKE

BETHANY SCOTT
HUNTSVILLE, AL

*This cake recipe has been passed down through generations. I
simplified it by subsituting the batter for cake mix. I find it to be most
like the original when I follow the egg white-only directions on the box
and beat them separtely; adding them in last. It's always best served
two days after it's made.*

**2 15-1/4-oz. pkg white
cake mix**

FILLING
8 large egg yolks
1-1/4 c. sugar
1/2 c. unsalted butter,
   softened
1/4 t. salt
1/2 c. bourbon
1 t. vanilla extract
1 c. raisins, finely
   chopped
1 c. pecans, finely
   chopped
1 c. grated coconut
1/2 c. candied fruit,
   finely chopped

FROSTING
2 T. plus 2 t. water
2 t. powdered
   unflavored gelatin
2 c. heavy whipping
   cream
1/2 c. powdered sugar
1 t. vanilla extract

Prepare cake mix batter according to directions on
box, using egg-white-only option, if available. Divide
batter evenly between four greaced and floured
9-inch round cake pans. Bake, cool and assemble
layers with filling between each layer, frost sides and
refridgerate cake for one-two days before serving.

Filling:
Place the egg yolks in a 2-quart saucepan and
lightly beat. Add sugar and beat until smooth. Add
butter and salt and cook over medium heat, stirring
constantly with a wooden spoon, until thick enough
to coat the back of the spoon, about 10 minutes.
Do not boil. Remove from heat and slowly stir in
bourbon and vanilla. Add chopped raisins, pecans,
coconut and candied fruit. Let cool.

Frosting:
Chill a large metal bowl and whisk attachment of
your mixer in the freezer. In a separate bowl, pour
water and sprinkle powdered gelatin over the water,
allowing gelatin to sit for 2 to 3 minutes. Microwave
the gelatin mixuture for 30 seconds in 10 second
intervals. set aside. In chilled bowl add cream,
powdered sugar and vanilla. Whip on high speed
until soft peaks form. Slowly add gelatin mixture and
whip on high speed until stiff peaks form.

NO-BAKE FRUITCAKE

CHRISTY BONNER
BERRY, AL

This recipe was handed down to me by my Great-Aunt Georgia. I love it because it's not your usual fruitcake. It's a real treat!

In a large bowl, combine graham crackers, cherries, raisins, coconut and pecans; set aside. In a medium saucepan over low heat, combine sweetened condensed milk and marshmallows. Stir until marshmallows are melted; pour over graham cracker mixture. Combine thoroughly. Press mixture into 3 wax paper-lined 9"x5" loaf pans. Cover and refrigerate until cool and rm. Remove from pans and slice.

Makes 3 loaves.

- 16-oz. pkg. graham crackers, crushed
- 2 c. candied red cherries, quartered
- 2 c. candied green cherries, quartered
- 2 c. raisins
- 2 c. sweetened flaked coconut
- 2 c. chopped pecans
- 14-oz. can sweetened condensed milk
- 16-oz. pkg. marshmallows

RICH HOT CHOCOLATE

KIMBERLY LITTLEFIELD
CENTRE, AL

We make this hot chocolate every Christmas Eve for our family. It is a "must-have" every year.

In a slow cooker, combine condensed milk, milk or water and vanilla. Add cocoa and salt; stir until smooth. Cover and cook on low setting for 4 hours, or on high setting for 2 hours, until very hot. Stir again. Ladle into mugs; top with marshmallows.

Makes 8 to 10 servings.

- 14-oz. can sweetened condensed milk
- 7-1/2 c. milk or water
- 1-1/2 t. vanilla extract
- 1/2 c. baking cocoa
- 1/8 t. salt
- Garnish: mini marshmallows

PUMPKIN BARS WITH CREAM CHEESE ICING

**KAY TURNER
SLOCUMB, AL**

This recipe has been a favorite in my family for 40 years! My children used to request it for their birthday cake. I decorate it for the season, adding a little orange coloring to the icing.

2 c. sugar
1 c. oil
4 eggs, beaten
2 c. canned pumpkin
2 c. all-purpose flour
2 t. baking powder
1 t. baking soda
1 t. cinnamon

CREAM CHEESE ICING:
8-oz. pkg. cream cheese,
1/2 c. butter
2 t. vanilla extract
   softened
3 c. powdered sugar

In a large bowl, mix together sugar, oil, eggs and pumpkin; mix well. Add remaining ingredients; stir well. Pour batter into a greased 15"x10" jelly-roll pan. Bake at 350 degrees about 45 minutes, until a toothpick tests done when inserted in the center. Cool; spread with Cream Cheese Icing. Cut into bars.

Makes 1-1/2 to 2 dozen.

Cream Cheese Icing:
In a bowl, blend together cream cheese, butter and vanilla. Gradually stir in enough powdered sugar to make a thick icing.

PRESENTATION

Dress up dessert! Drizzle hot fudge or caramel sauce from a squeeze bottle, on plates prior to plating the dessert.

NUTTY CRANBERRY SNACK MIX

JOANN
GOOSEBERRY PATCH

This is one of the first treats requested in our house at Christmas-time!

Combine cereal and walnuts in a large microwave-safe bowl; set aside. In a microwave-safe bowl, combine orange juice concentrate, brown sugar and oil. Microwave, uncovered, on high for one minute; stir. Microwave for one minute longer, stirring after 30 seconds, until hot. Pour over cereal mixture; stir until evenly coated. Microwave on high for 5 minutes, stirring every 2 minutes. Stir in cranberries. Spread on wax paper or aluminum foil to cool. Store in a tightly covered container.

Makes 8 cups.

6 c. bite-size crispy rice cereal squares with cinnamon

1 c. walnut halves

1/4 c. frozen orange juice concentrate, thawed

1/4 c. brown sugar, packed

2 T. oil

1/2 c. sweetened dried cranberries

SIMPLY SWEET

RENEE SUITS
MCCALLA, AL

My husband's grandfather just loved this dessert. He would always ask me if I was going to fix it for a holiday meal. We caught him one year hiding small amounts around the kitchen!

Combine whipped topping and gelatin in a large bowl; add fruit. Stir in one cup nuts; mix until well blended. Sprinkle with remaining nuts; refrigerate until ready to serve.

Makes 6 to 8 servings.

16-oz. container frozen whipped topping, thawed

6-oz. pkg. favorite-flavor gelatin mix

1-1/2 c. chopped nuts, divided

15-oz. can fruit cocktail, drained

BETTY'S LEMON PIE

ALLISON HAYES
JEMISON, AL

This recipe came from my grandmother, Betty. It's the easiest, most delicious treat! I hope you will enjoy this family recipe.

8-oz. pkg. cream cheese, softened

14-oz. can sweetened condensed milk

juice of 2 lemons

9-inch graham cracker pie crust

For best results, let cream cheese soften at room temperature for 3 hours. Combine cream cheese, condensed milk and lemon juice in a large bowl. Beat with an electric mixer on medium speed until mixture is smooth. Pour into crust. Cover and chill for 4 hours before serving. Cut into wedges.

Makes 8 servings.

STRAWBERRY SHORTCAKES

VICKIE
GOOSEBERRY PATCH

For a special treat, dust each serving with a little baking cocoa.

2 pts. strawberries, hulled and sliced

2/3 c. plus 1/4 c. sugar, divided

2-1/3 c. biscuit baking mix

3 T. butter, melted

1/2 c. milk

3/4 c. whipping cream, whipped

Sprinkle strawberries with 2/3 cup sugar; let stand for one hour. Combine baking mix, 3 tablespoons sugar, butter and milk until a soft dough forms. Drop by tablespoonfuls into 6 mounds on an ungreased baking sheet; sprinkle with remaining sugar. Bake at 425 degrees for 10 to 12 minutes. Beat whipping cream in a chilled bowl until stiff. Split shortcakes in half; spoon strawberries between halves and tops. Top with whipped cream.

Serves 6.

PUMPKIN SWIRL BREAD

JENNY SHRIDER
DAPHNE, AL

This is a delicious bread that we make every Thanksgiving. It's very easy to make, and your kids will love helping!

In a large bowl, combine flour, sugar, baking soda, spices and salt; mix well. Add remaining ingredients; stir until moistened. Reserve 1-3/4 cups batter. Pour remaining batter into a well-greased 9"x5" loaf pan. Top with Filling; add reserved batter. Cut through batter several times with a knife for a swirl effect. Bake at 350 degrees for one hour and 20 minutes, or until bread tests done with a toothpick. Cool 10 minutes; remove from pan.

Makes one loaf.

Filling:
Blend cream cheese and sugar. Add egg and mix well.

1-3/4 c. all-purpose flour
1-1/2 c. sugar
1 t. baking soda
1 t. cinnamon
1/4 t. nutmeg
1/2 t. salt
1 c. canned pumpkin
1/2 c. margarine, melted
1 egg, beaten
1/3 c. water

FILLING:
8-oz. pkg. cream cheese,
1/4 c. sugar softened
1 egg, beaten

KITCHEN TIP

Add to the storage life of your uncooked potatoes by adding a few whole apples in with the potatoes.

INDEX

INDEX continued

U.S. to **METRIC RECIPE EQUIVALENTS**

¼ teaspoon . . . . 1 mL
½ teaspoon . . . . 2 mL
1 teaspoon . . . . 5 mL
1 tablespoon = 3 teaspoons . . . . . . 15 mL
2 tablespoons = 1 fluid ounce . . . . 30 mL
¼ cup . . . . 60 mL
⅓ cup . . . . 75 mL
½ cup = 4 fluid ounces . . . . 125 mL
1 cup = 8 fluid ounces . . . . 250 mL
2 cups = 1 pint = 16 fluid ounces 500 mL
4 cups = 1 quart . . . . 1 L

1 ounce . . . . 30 g
4 ounces . . . . 120 g
8 ounces . . . . 225 g
16 ounces = 1 pound . . . . 450 g

Square
8x8x2 inches . . . . 2 L = 20x20x5 cm
9x9x2 inches . . . . . . 2.5 L = 23x23x5 cm

Rectangular
13x9x2 inches . . . . . 3.5 L = 33x23x5 cm

Loaf
9x5x3 inches . . . . 2 L = 23x13x7 cm

Round
8x1½ inches . . . . 1.2 L = 20x4 cm
9x1½ inches . . . . 1.5 L = 23x4 cm

t. = teaspoon . . . . ltr. = liter
T. = tablespoon . . . . oz. = ounce
c. = cup . . . . lb. = pound
pt. = pint . . . . doz. = dozen
qt. = quart . . . . pkg. = package
gal. = gallon . . . . env. = envelope

300° F . . . . .150° C
325° F . . . . .160° C
350° F . . . . .180° C
375° F . . . . .190° C
400° F . . . . .200° C
450° F . . . . .230° C

A pinch = ⅛ tablespoon
1 fluid ounce = 2 tablespoons
3 teaspoons = 1 tablespoon
4 fluid ounces = ½ cup
2 tablespoons = ⅛ cup
8 fluid ounces = 1 cup
4 tablespoons = ¼ cup
16 fluid ounces = 1 pint
8 tablespoons = ½ cup
32 fluid ounces = 1 quart
16 tablespoons = 1 cup
16 ounces net weight = 1 pound
2 cups = 1 pint
4 cups = 1 quart
4 quarts = 1 gallon

Send us your favorite recipe

and the memory that makes it special for you!*

If we select your recipe for a brand-new **Gooseberry Patch** cookbook, your name will appear right along with it...and you'll receive a FREE copy of the book!

Submit your recipe on our website at

www.gooseberrypatch.com/sharearecipe

*Please include the number of servings and all other necessary information.

Have a taste for more?

Visit www.gooseberrypatch.com to join our Circle of Friends!

• Free recipes, tips and ideas plus a complete cookbook index
• Get mouthwatering recipes and special email offers delivered to your inbox.

You'll also love these cookbooks from **Gooseberry Patch**!

A Year Of Holidays
Christmas for Sharing
Classic Church Potlucks
Farmhouse Kitchen
Our Best Cast-Iron Cooking Recipes
Our Best Recipes from Grandma's Cookie Jar
Quick & Easy Recipes with Help
Shortcuts to Grandma's Best Recipes
Slow Cookers, Casseroles & Skillets
Welcome Autumn

www.gooseberrypatch.com